QUMRAN
STUDIES

QUMRAN STUDIES

CHAIM RABIN

SCHOCKEN BOOKS · NEW YORK

First SCHOCKEN PAPERBACK edition 1975

Copyright © 1957 Oxford University Press

Published by arrangement with the Clarendon Press Oxford

Library of Congress Cataloging in Publication Data

Rabin, Chaim.
  Qumran studies.

  Includes bibliographical references.
  1. Qumran community. 2. Judaism—Relations—Islam. 3. Islam—Relations—
Judaism. I. Title. II. Series: Scripta Judaica; 2.
BM175.Q6R3   1975   296.8′1   74-26735

Manufactured in the United States of America

TO

G. R. DRIVER

PREFACE

CHAPTERS I–VII of this book are an enlarged version of three lectures delivered at the University of Durham under the terms of the Jacobson Lectureship in Jewish Studies; Chapter VIII is based on a lecture given at the Institute of Jewish Studies in Manchester. The thread that holds them together is the attempt to test an alternative to the theory that the Dead Sea Scrolls emanate from the Essene community. This theory appears to be almost universally accepted, and has led to widespread and somewhat unexpected consequences. Not only are ever larger sections of the Pseud-epigraphal literature being attributed to Essene authors, but we already hear of an 'Essene Bible text' and the 'Essene scribal art'. It is thus all the more important to give the fullest consideration to other possibilities of identification of the Qumran sect.

I am not breaking entirely new ground in connecting the Scrolls with Pharisaism. One year after the publication of the *Zadokite Fragments* by Schechter, W. H. Ward drew attention to some points of contact with the Pharisees (*Bibliotheca Sacra* lxviii. 429–56), and in the same year the late Prof. L. Ginzberg began his series of articles in the *MGWJ*, later incorporated in his *Eine unbekannte jüdische Sekte*, where the identity of 'Zadokite' halakhah with the Pharisee-Rabbinic system is demonstrated in detail. Since the discovery of the Dead Sea Scrolls, Ginzberg's view seems to have found no following, except for a somewhat hesitant suggestion in 1950 by Père de Vaux (*RB* lvii. 428), although Ginzberg's book has been widely quoted.

In comparing features of the Qumran sect with Pharisaism, I have endeavoured to distinguish clearly between Pharisaism and Rabbinic Judaism as represented by Tannaitic literature. If my theory should find some acceptance, then the Scrolls would become a source for gaining a better insight into the distinctive features of the earlier group, and thus their importance for the history of Judaism would be increased. It is just for this reason that I have concentrated on those aspects in which a distinction between Pharisaism and Rabbinic Judaism can be established without the help of the Scrolls, and have in particular refrained from discussing theological beliefs, except the comparatively clear-cut matter of bodily resurrection. If the points discussed are relatively unimportant, all the better, for it is such points where independent parallel developments are least likely and where the bias of later sources, because of their unimportance, has had less effect.

The broad outline of the theory advanced is that the Qumran community continues the *haburah* of the first century B.C., an organization within which people could trust each other in matters of tithing of produce, ritual purity of food, and other halakhic matters affecting everyday contact between individuals. The Qumran community—in this view—represents the old haburah more faithfully than does the 'Rabbinic' community of the Tannaitic period, because the latter had made extensive concessions in halakhic matters in order to enable non-Pharisees to share in its life. These concessions were largely the reason for the schism, though personal quarrels may have played a certain role in bringing it about. At first the Qumran group simply maintained, according to its lights, the original Pharisaic organization and practice; as time went on it may well have adopted practices of its own to differentiate it further from the Rabbinic majority (e.g. its own calendar, cf. Chapter V), while at the same time the haburah organization, with all it entailed, withered away in Rabbinic Judaism, and the Law was rapidly further developed to meet changing circumstances. Each of the two, the Qumran sect and Rabbinic Judaism, saw itself as the real heir of the great Pharisee tradition. The Qumran sect got the worst of the struggle and, as far as we know, its literature only survived in the outpost by the Dead Sea where part or all of the group dwelt at one stage in its history for reasons unknown to us.

My theory, by placing the rise of the Qumran community at the point of transition between Pharisaism and Rabbinic Judaism, requires a dating within the first century A.D. I have not attempted to define the date more closely, nor have I proposed any identifications for the various personalities mentioned in the Scrolls. If we accept the archaeologists' reasons for dating the final abandonment of Khirbet Qumran by the sect in A.D. 69, we might perhaps identify the sect with the people who reoccupied the main building after 4 B.C. (we do not know how long after). They may well have returned to a place formerly inhabited (from the time of John Hyrcanus, 135–104 B.C., to the beginning of Herod's reign, 37 B.C.) by other Pharisees, part of the main body of that sect. Perhaps the foundation of this desert refuge was connected with the persecution of the Pharisees by John Hyrcanus.

I make no apologies for including the more speculative chapter on 'Islam and the Qumran Sect'. It is founded, like the rest, on the identification of the Scrolls sect as a diehard Pharisee group, and the theory propounded in it would, if accepted, bring further support for that identification.

It is a pleasant duty for me to thank Rabbi Dr. A. Altmann for publishing the book in the series edited by him, Prof. T. W. Thacker for permitting me to publish my Durham lectures in this form, the members of the Oriental faculty at Durham who made our stay there such a memorable occasion for us, Professor Sir Hamilton Gibb for his encouragement and advice in connexion with Chapter VIII, Professor J. Schacht and Dr. E. J. Z. Werblowsky for valuable criticism, and my wife for her precious and willing assistance in getting this book ready.

I also wish to express my gratitude to the Board of Directors of the Conference on Jewish Material Claims against Germany, Inc., New York, for their grant to the Institute of Jewish Studies in support of this publication.

C. R.

Oxford
September 1956

CONTENTS

ABBREVIATIONS

AJSLL	*American Journal of Semitic Languages and Literatures*
Ant.	*Antiquitates Judaeorum*
Aq.	Aquilas
AZ	'Abodah Zarah
Bacher, *Tannaiten*	*Die Agada der Tannaiten*, 1884–90
BB	Baba Bathra
Bekh.	Bekhoroth
Ber.	Berakhoth
BH	Biblical Hebrew
BJ	*Bellum Judaicum*
BJRL	*Bulletin of the John Rylands Library*
BM	Baba Meẓi'a
BQ	Baba Qamma
Brownlee, *Manual*	*The Dead Sea Manual of Discipline*, BASOR Suppl. Studies, x–xii (1951)
B.T.	Babylonian Talmud
CDC	The Zadokite or Damascus Document
DSD	The Discipline Scroll
DSD i*, &c.	Parts of DSD publ. in *QC I*, pp. 109–11 (= 1QSa)
DSH	Pesher Habakkuk
DSIa	Isaiah Scroll A (publ. New Haven, 1950)
DSIb	Isaiah Scroll B (publ. in *Oẓar ha-Megilloth ha-Genuzoth*, ed. E. L. Sukenik, Jerusalem, 1956)
DST	The Thanksgiving Scroll
DSW	The War of the Sons of Light and the Sons of Darkness
Edu.	'Eduyoth
Enc. Isl.	*Encyclopaedia of Islam*
Eru.	'Erubin
Ginzberg, *Legends*	*Legends of the Jews*, 1909
Git.	Giṭṭin
Hag.	Ḥagigah
Heb.	Hebrew
HUCA	Hebrew Union College Annual
Hul.	Ḥullin

J.	Journal
JBL	*Journal of Biblical Literature*
JJS	*Journal of Jewish Studies*
JQR	*Jewish Quarterly Review*
Ket.	Kethubboth
M.	Mishnah
Maas.	Ma'aseroth
Makk.	Makkoth
Meg.	Megillah
Mekh.	Mekhilta
Men.	Menaḥoth
MGWJ	*Monatsschrift für die Geschichte und Wissenschaft des Judentums*
MH	Mishnaic Hebrew
MSh.	Ma'aser Sheni
Naz.	Nazir
Ned.	Nedarim
Nid.	Niddah
Ohol.	Oholoth
PAAJR	*Proceedings of the American Academy for Jewish Research*
PEQ	*Palestine Exploration Quarterly*
Pes.	Pesaḥin
Pesh.	Peshitta
PMic.	Pesher Micah (publ. in *QC I*, pp. 77–79)
PNa.	Pesher Nahum (publ. in *JBL* lxxv (1956), 89–93)
PPs. 37	Pesher Psalm 37 (publ. in *PEQ* 1955, pp. 69–75; parts publ. in *JBL* lxxv (1956), 94–95, are cited with the *JBL* reference)
P.T.	Palestinian Talmud
P.-W.	Pauly-Wissowa, *Real-Enzyklopädie des klassischen Altertums*
QC I	*Qumran Cave I*, ed. Barthélemy and Milik, Oxford, 1955
Qid.	Qiddushin
Rabb.	Rabbinic
RB	*Revue Biblique*
RÉJ	*Revue des Études Juives*
RSh.	Rosh Hashanah
San.	Sanhedrin

Schürer	*Geschichte des jüdischen Volkes im Zeitalter Jesu Christi*, 4th German edn., 1901
seq.	and following pages or numbers
Shab.	Shabbath
Sheb.	Shebi'ith
Sheq.	Sheqalim
Sot.	Soṭah
Suk.	Sukkah
Syr.	Syriac
Targ.	Targum
Tem.	Temurah
Tg.	Targum
Tg. Jer.	Targum Jerushalmi
Theod.	Theodotion
TJ	Targum Jonathan
Tos.	Tosephta
T.S.	*Tě'ězāza Sanbat*
vs.	verse
VT	*Vetus Testamentum*
Vulg.	Vulgate
Yadin	*Měgillath Milḥemeth běnē or bi-věnē ḥoshekh*, Jerusalem, 1955
Yeb.	Yebamoth
Zab.	Zabim
ZD	*The Zadokite Documents*, ed. C. Rabin, Oxford, 1954
ZDMG	*Zeitschrift der Deutschen Morgenländischen Gesellschaft*
Zeb.	Zebaḥim

TRANSLITERATION OF HEBREW

No distinction is made between long and short vowels. The sign ⌣ marks Shewa mobile and Hatephs, no distinction being made between Shewa mobile and Hateph Segol. At the end of a word, $\bar{e} = Zer\bar{e}\text{-}yodh$, $\bar{a} = Qama\underline{z}\text{-}Aleph$.

Dagesh forte is marked by doubling. Dagesh lene and Raphe:

b—v	k—kh
g—gh	p—f
d—dh	t—th

Raphe, however, is sometimes ignored where an accepted spelling exists, e.g. *haber, haburah*.

QUMRAN
STUDIES

I

THE NOVITIATE

ONE of the most characteristic and distinctive features of every organization is its method of filling its ranks. The constitutions of clubs and societies are mostly devoted to fixing the rules of this process in great detail. Since the exact procedure is only indirectly related to the ideology and purposes of the group, accidents in its history and the whim of leading members play an important part in the formation of such rules, which therefore constitute a convenient 'tracer element' in assigning documents to their correct origins.

Fortunately we are not only well informed about the procedure the Qumran sect employed in admitting new members, but possess also valuable information on the rules observed in this matter by the Essenes and by the Pharisee haburah. The sect's custom is clearly set out in DSD vi. 13–23. The text is here reproduced in a modernized orthography, to fit in with the Tiberian vocalization, and divided into verses:

1. וְכָל־הַמִּתְנַדֵּב מִיִּשְׂרָאֵל לְהִנָּסֵף עַל־עֲצַת הַיַּחַד יִדְרְשֵׁהוּ¹ הָאִישׁ הַפָּקִיד בְּרֹאשׁ הָרַבִּים לְשִׂכְלוֹ וּלְמַעֲשָׂיו: 2. וְאִם־יַשִּׂיג מוּסָר יְבִיאֵהוּ בַּבְּרִית לָשׁוּב לָאֱמֶת וְלָסוּר מִכָּל־עָוֶל וִיבִינֵהוּ בְּכָל־מִשְׁפְּטֵי הַיָּחַד: 3. וְאַחַר בְּבוֹאוֹ לַעֲמֹד לִפְנֵי הָרַבִּים וְנִשְׁאֲלוּ הַכֹּל עַל־דְּבָרָיו וְכַאֲשֶׁר יֵצֵא הַגּוֹרָל עַל־עֲצַת הָרַבִּים יִקְרַב אוֹ יִרְחָק: 4. וּבְקָרְבוֹ לַעֲצַת הַיַּחַד לֹא־יִגַּע בְּטָהֳרַת הָרַבִּים עַד־אֲשֶׁר יִדְרְשׁוּהוּ לְרוּחוֹ וּלְמַעֲשָׂיו עַד־מְלֹאת־לוֹ שָׁנָה תְמִימָה: 5. וְגַם־הוּא אַל־יִתְעָרֵב בְּהוֹן הָרַבִּים: 6. וּבִמְלֹאת־לוֹ שָׁנָה בְּתוֹךְ הַיַּחַד וְשָׁאֲלוּ הָרַבִּים עַל־דְּבָרָיו לְפִי שִׂכְלוֹ וּמַעֲשָׂיו בַּתּוֹרָה: 7. וְאִם־יֵצֵא־לוֹ הַגּוֹרָל לִקְרַב לְסוֹד הַיַּחַד עַל־פִּי הַכֹּהֲנִים וְרֹב אַנְשֵׁי בְרִיתָם יְקָרְבוּ גַם אֶת־הוֹנוֹ וְאֶת־מְלַאכְתּוֹ אֶל־יַד הָאִישׁ הַמְבַקֵּר עַל־מְלֶאכֶת הָרַבִּים: 8. וּכְתָבוֹ בְּחֶשְׁבּוֹן בְּיָדוֹ וְעַל־הָרַבִּים אַל־יוֹצִיאֶנּוּ: 9. אַל־יִגַּע בְּמַשְׁקֵה הָרַבִּים עַד־מְלֹאת־לוֹ שָׁנָה שֵׁנִית בְּתוֹךְ אַנְשֵׁי הַיַּחַד: 10. וּבִמְלֹאת־לוֹ הַשָּׁנָה הַשֵּׁנִית יִפְקְדוּהוּ עַל־פִּי הָרַבִּים: 11. וְאִם־יֵצֵא־לוֹ הַגּוֹרָל לְקָרְבוֹ לַיַּחַד יִכְתְּבֻהוּ בְּסֶרֶךְ תְּכוּנוֹ תִּכּוּנוֹ בְתוֹךְ אֶחָיו לַתּוֹרָה וְלַמִּשְׁפָּט וְלַטָּהֳרָה וּלְעָרֵב אֶת־הוֹנוֹ וִיהִי עֲצָתוֹ לַיַּחַד וּמִשְׁפָּטוֹ:

¹ MS. ‏ידורשהו‏.

Translation

1. And everyone of Israel who volunteers to join the Council of the Community shall be examined by the man appointed at the head of the Many about his intelligence and his actions.

2. And if he is able to benefit from instruction,[1] he shall bring him[2] into the covenant to return to the truth and to depart from all injustice, and shall instruct him in all the statutes of the Community.

3. And afterwards, when he comes to stand before the Many, all shall be asked concerning him; and as the ballot turns out in the Council of the Many, so shall he approach or be kept away.

4. And when he approaches the Council of the Community, he shall not touch the Purity of the Many until they have examined him about his spirit and his actions, until a full year has been completed by him.

5. Furthermore[3] he shall not 'mingle' with the property of the Many.

6. And when he has completed a year within the Community, they shall ask the Many concerning him according to his intelligence and his actions in the Law.

7. And if the ballot turns out for him to approach the Council[4] of the Community by the decision of the priests and the majority of their associates, they shall cause to approach also his property and his work to the hand of the man who is overseer over the work of the Many.

8. And he shall write it down in the (*or* with) reckoning with his own hand, but to the Many he shall not bring it out.

9. Let him not touch the Drink of the Many until he has completed a second year amongst the men of the Community.

10. And when he has completed the second year, they shall muster him according to the decision of the Many.

11. And if the ballot turns out for him to approach to the

---

[1] Cf. CDC vi. 10.
[2] Or—as the scrolls sometimes omit *waw* before this suffix—'they shall bring him'.
[3] A Biblicizing adaptation of Mishnaic Hebrew *af hu*.
[4] The meaning 'mystery' is unlikely; see below, p. 9.

Community, they shall[1] write him down in the arrangement of his (numerical) order[2] amongst his brothers for Law and judgement and Purity and to 'mingle' his property, and let his counsel and his judgement benefit the Community.

The initiation of the new member thus takes place in four distinct stages:

A. The examination before the man appointed at the head of the Many.

This concludes with 'bringing him into the covenant' and results in his being taught all the statutes.

B. After an indefinite time, the consultation of the Many.

We are told only what this does not entitle him to, namely either to touch the Purity or to 'mingle' with the communal property.

C. After one year, a detailed examination of his 'intelligence and actions in the Law'. The decision is now made not by the Many, but by the 'priests and their associates'.

Presumably he is now allowed to touch the Purity and to 'mingle' with the property of the Many. His own property and labour are carefully recorded by an official, but not 'brought out unto the Many'. He still is excluded from the 'drink'.

D. After a further year, he is 'mustered', the decision this time being in the hands of the Many.

The result is complete 'brotherhood', including the 'mingling' of his property. He is given a status ('numerical order') in the Community: this not only makes him a member of one of the military units described in DSW, but also is a necessary preliminary for giving of his 'counsel and judgement' in the assembly, where everyone is asked in strict order (CDC xiv. 6) and no one must speak out of turn (DSD vi. 10[3]).

We may thus speak of a pre-novitiate (A) of indefinite duration, followed by a novitiate of two years, with an intermediate examination in the middle.

---

[1] Or 'he shall . . .'.   [2] Cf. ἐκόσμησεν for *tikken* in Ecclus. xlii. 21.

[3] Where at the end of line 10 *lifnē* should be supplied before *ha-kathuv*.

For the pre-novitiate, we have a second text, CDC xv. 7–11: 'And the same applies to everyone who during the whole epoch of wickedness turns from his corrupt way: on the day that he speaks with the overseer of the Many, they shall muster him with the oath of the covenant which Moses concluded with Israel, namely the covenant to return to the Law of Moses with all his heart and with all his soul, namely to that which has been discovered[1] so as to be done in the whole epoch of wickedness. And no man shall let him know the statutes until he has stood before the overseer, lest he turn out to be a fool when he examines him.'

We may assume that in spite of the difference in name the same official is meant. He is, as CDC xiv. 5–6 shows, a priest, and we may conclude from his mention immediately after the procedure of voting that he was a kind of chairman of the meeting of the Many. This agrees with his task here: he, so to say, prepares a file for the assembly, eliminating the unlikely candidates and apparently reporting to the Many, since nothing is said about a further examination at the end of the pre-novitiate; only a decision is made.

Clearly the sect only accepted members of a certain intellectual standard. Apart from the two passages quoted, this is borne out by DSD i*. 19–22: 'And any foolish man shall not come into the lot so as to set himself up[2] over the congregation of Israel for contending and for judgement and to bear the burden of the community. . . .'[3] However, it is doubtful whether *śekhel* here means in fact general intelligence. If it did, the renewed examination of the novice's *śekhel* at stage C (vs. 6) would be pointless, as it would hardly be likely to produce any results different from those of the inquiry at stage A. It is also difficult to imagine how the Many in a public session could have investigated a man's intelligence quotient. The phrase 'intelligence and actions' recalls the Rabbinic 'study and actions' (e.g. Aboth 1. 17), and this suggests that *śekhel* here means 'religious knowledge'.[4] It may well be that in

---

[1] On the language, see pp. 99–100.

[2] Cf. CDC x. 8.

[3] CDC xiii. 6 envisages the case of a priest within the sectarian community being 'a fool'. Possibly the intellectual test was not applied to those born within the sect.

[4] In DSD ix. 12 it seems to mean the total of religious knowledge possessed by the sect.

verse 6 the words 'in the Law' belong both to 'his intelligence' and 'his actions'.

The different degrees of religious knowledge also determined the position of a member within a given group. CDC xiii. 11 deals with the admission of a new member, who is already a 'brother' of the sect, into a local group, or 'camp'. He is examined 'about his actions and his intelligence and his strength and his courage and his property, and they shall write him down in his place according to his status in the lot of light'; his placing within the new group might of course be different from that in his former local branch. Note that here he is examined about his military prowess, too, since the units of the sect are also military units, but the neophyte is at no stage examined about his prowess. This is particularly interesting in comparison with the Essenes, who tested their neophytes for ἐγκράτεια and καρτερία, self-control and endurance (*BJ* II. viii. 7).

No such tests were apparently made with children of members, who had, however, to take an oath (CDC xv. 5–6) when attaining the age of twenty; it is not clear whether thereafter they had to pass through the two years of the novitiate. This may be the explanation of the curious fact that any military service begins only at the age of twenty-five years,[1] and that the *na'ar za'aṭuṭ* below that age is forbidden to enter the battle encampment—just as all women are (DSW vii. 3)—possibly as not possessing the necessary degree of ritual purity.

The preliminary examination is followed by an oath. DSD makes it absolutely clear that the 'covenant' comes after the examination. On the other hand the words 'on the day that he speaks to the overseer' in CDC show that the oath was taken immediately after the successful examination. The obligation undertaken by the oath was to 'return to the Law of Moses' (CDC xv. 9; xvi. 1–2, 5–6; DSD v. 8).[2] It is apparently based upon Neh. x. 30, and, as there, it is also a 'covenant' (*ămanah*), though concluded by each member separately. A much broken passage

---

[1] Cf. the table in Yadin, ch. 5, para. 4.
[2] Mentioned DST xiv. 17: 'and with an oath I have imposed upon myself not to sin against Thee'.

in CDC xv. 12–13 seems to state that retribution for sins can be exacted from the moment this oath has been performed.

In particular the entrant undertakes, according to CDC, to keep 'that which is discovered to be done during the whole epoch of wickedness', i.e. the special laws which the sect has worked out in order to preserve the practice of the Law as far as the difficult present time allows. These, the special sectarian laws, are no doubt the 'statutes' (*mishpaṭim*) which no one is allowed to reveal to the neophyte before he has taken the oath.[1]

It is true that the Essenes also demanded 'terrible oaths'[2] from neophytes (*BJ* ii. viii. 7), promising 'not to discover any of their doctrines to others, even though tortured to death'. Apart from the fact that this came at the *end* of the Essene novitiate, it is evidently of a different character. The Qumran sect is simply warned not to reveal the 'statutes' too early to a new member; no grave sin is implied. Also the member of a haburah was forbidden to give an Am-Haarez straightforward instruction on matters of ritual purity (Tos. Demai 2. 24), this being a subject intimately connected with the practice of the haburah; by implication we may assume that one was allowed to instruct an Am-Haarez about other religious laws.

Having studied the 'statutes of the Community' to their full extent, the neophyte appears before the Many. This term covers the group as a social entity, as opposed to the individual,[3] but it may in this connexion stand for the 'session of the Many', the procedure of which is discussed in the lines immediately preceding the section of DSD here discussed, and which is probably identical with the 'session of the cities of Israel', CDC xii. 20, and the 'session of all camps', ibid. xiv. 3, i.e. the periodical central council. If this was also the occasion on which the blessing-and-

---

[1] True, CDC only says 'until he has stood before the overseer', but as the examination and the oath seem to have taken place at the same sitting, this would imply that he has also sworn.

[2] Bauer, *P.-W. Suppl.* iv. 425, rightly points out that the Essenes refrained from oaths, but this does not justify his conclusion that the information is wrong. On the contrary, their reticence made this one oath all the more impressive. The same applies to the Qumran sect, who also avoided oaths, cf. CDC xv. 1–5.

[3] It is worth stressing that 'the Many' is quite a common Rabbinic term. See p. 17, n. 2.

curse ceremony of DSD i–ii was performed 'year by year' (ii. 19), this would be the easiest explanation for the annual intervals between the three reconsiderations of each applicant, and would also account for the indeterminate length of the pre-novitiate period, which was simply the time until the next annual session.

What happened to those who had been accepted by the overseer and taught, but failed to pass the scrutiny of the Many? There must have been a number of such people who had sworn the oath and were therefore answerable for their religious behaviour, and yet were not allowed 'to touch the Purity of the Many'. Indeed, the sect itself added to this circle by its practice of excluding from the Purity those who had committed crimes but could not be properly convicted because of an insufficient number of witnesses (CDC ix. 20–23). So were also people who had not kept their undertakings implied in the oath (DSD v. 13), who had lied about property (ibid. vi. 25), had spoken in anger to a priest of those 'registered in the book' (vii. 3), or generally rebelled against the law of the sect (vii. 19). Such people were in fact not ejected from the community: the very fact that they were at the same time 'punished'[1] shows that they continued to be under its discipline. In the two last-mentioned passages the duration of the state of relegation is one year, i.e.—if our surmise about the assembly is right—from the meeting which condemned them until the next one.

It was thus possible to live for a considerable period 'within the Community' (vs. 6) without touching the Purity or 'mingling' with the property of the Many. It is most unlikely that Purity means the ritual bath. A properly appointed ritual bath cannot be made impure; that this Rabbinic view was also held by the Qumran sect is clearly shown by CDC x. 12–13. Ritual baths in certain circumstances were incumbent upon everybody, and the sect could hardly have prevented its neophytes from fulfilling their religious duty, all the more so as this would have exposed the other members who had to be in contact with the neophyte—e.g. his teacher—to constant danger of uncleanness by contact. The key is provided by DSD v. 13: 'let him not enter the water so as to touch the Purity of the men of holiness'. Here the 'water' and the

---

[1] For the meaning of this, see Ch. II, p. 26.

touching of the Purity are clearly distinguished; the ritual bath is the preliminary to touching the Purity. This can only mean that the Purity is ritually pure food, the *ṭohŏroth* of the Rabbis. The Qumran sectarians were *okhĕlē ḥullin bĕ-ṭohŏrah*, men who ate ordinary food with all the ritual precautions which priests had to employ when eating of the heave-offering. Such food became impure through contact with an impure person, and letting it become impure was in itself sinful—even if the pure person did not afterwards eat it—so that we learn that it was forbidden to send such pure food through an Am-Haareẓ or feed it to one (Tos. Demai 2. 20–21). Amongst the Essenes, too, the novice is not allowed to touch the common food (*BJ* II. viii. 7). The preparation of the common food was by the Essenes entrusted to priests (*Ant.* XVIII. i. 5); Rabbinic sources refer to the habit of inviting priests to process oil and other victuals liable to receive uncleanness.[1]

The pure food is specified as 'the Purity of the Many'. If we remember that 'the Many' always refers to a body, we see that the term here means common meals, from which the applicant and the first-year novice are excluded, though living 'within' the community. There was thus also food apart from the common meals, and such food was not of such a kind as to be considered 'pure things' which must not be handed to an impure person. The simplest explanation is, of course, that this food, which the novice ate during the first year, was his own.

We shall deal in Chapter II[2] with the term 'mingling' with regard to the property of the Many.

After this first year, the novice again appears before the Many. The final decision, however, at this stage is not taken by the whole body, but by 'the priests and their associates'. These, I would suggest, are none other than the 'judges of the congregation' of CDC x. 5, a body composed of four of the tribe of Levi and Aaron and six Israelites. These were also an administrative body, collaborating with the overseer in the financial affairs of the sect (CDC xiv. 13). Since the last-mentioned regulation appears under the heading 'And this is the procedure of the Many to prepare all their requirements', one wonders whether the 'judges' were not an

---

[1] Büchler, p. 156.   [2] pp. 27–31.

organ of the central 'session of the Many', i.e. there was only one set of 'judges' within the community.

The body to which he is now allowed to 'approach' is called *sodh*, while in stage B he was taken into the *'eẓah*. There may be some significance in the difference of terminology, but the two words seem elsewhere to be interchangeable, and there is in the style of the scrolls a distinct tendency towards elegant variation.

We may take it that he was now permitted to touch the Purity of the Many, i.e. partake of the common meals, but he is still excluded from the 'drink' of the Many. As is well known, Rabbinic law, based on Lev. xi. 38, considers fluids conveyors of uncleanness. A person whose presence near dry food may not contaminate it endangers the purity of a fluid or of wet food. The point is neatly illustrated by Tos. Demai 6. 8: if an Am-Haareẓ dies, leaving two sons, of whom one is a haber and one an Am-Haareẓ, 'the haber may eat all the dry food but must burn all the wet food that has fallen to his share'.

Of course, the prohibition of touching here only refers to the 'drink of the Many', i.e. the wine over which a blessing was recited before the meal (DSD vi. 5; ii*. 17 seq.) and which thus was given only to full members.

At this stage, by implication, the novice is allowed to 'mingle' with the property of the Many. His own property and labour are 'brought close' and registered, as a preparatory stage for the 'mingling' which takes place after he becomes a full member. See further, Chapter II.

The decision after the second year of novitiate is again entirely that of the Many. If 'brought near', he is admitted to the drink of the Many, his property is 'mingled', and he becomes a member with full vote, giving of his 'counsel and judgement'.

The term used for successfully passing the different stages, 'to approach', is also Rabbinic, and occurs in the regulations about the haburah.

We may now compare this procedure with that of the Essenes, as described by Josephus in *BJ* II. viii. 7. Josephus claims (*Vita* 2) to have passed through the 'three courses' himself, i.e. at least to have gone through the Essene novitiate. Even if he was unsuccessful in being finally accepted, he must have been acquainted with the conditions imposed on novices, and, being a Pharisee, must have been able to compare the special duties and restrictions imposed with those incumbent upon a Pharisee, i.e. he was in a situation not unlike our own, who compare Essenism with Rabbinic Judaism. We may therefore take his statements at their face value, even if we suspect him of misreporting conditions in the inner order itself.

A. One year of pre-novitiate, during which the applicant remains outside. He is given a hatchet, a loin cloth, and white garments, and is required to live in the same way as the Essenes. This gives evidence of his self-control.

B. A period of two years, during which he is 'brought nearer' to their way of life, and his character ($\tilde{\eta}\theta os$) is tested.

During this period he is not yet received into their $\sigma\upsilon\mu\beta\iota\dot\omega\sigma\epsilon\iota s$ and not allowed to touch the common food, but is allowed the use of their 'purer water'.

C. The administration of 'tremendous oaths' before admission to full membership. As para. 8 shows, those expelled from the order for serious crimes do not violate the 'oaths and usages', even to the point of death.

Similarities between the procedure of the Essenes and the Qumran sect:

1. The Essene novitiate is three years, at Qumran probably a maximum of three years.

2. There is a pre-novitiate stage of (maximum) one year's duration.

3. The progress of the novice is expressed in increasing reliance on his ritual purity.

Doubtful points:

1. As described in *BJ*, the Essene novitiate proper lasts two years without any further division. However, if we assume Josephus not to have reached full membership, he may have been ignorant of further subdivisions.

2. We have merely assumed that in stage B (corresponding to the Essene second year) the Qumran novice was admitted to

the ritual baths. With the Essenes he is permitted to use them after the first year.

3. The pre-novitiate is for the Essene applicant a test whether he can stand the rigorous life of the order, for the Qumran novice a period of legal study. On the other hand the Qumran novice was of course expected to practise what he learnt, and his 'actions' were watched; the Essene aspirant had to learn something of their 'way of life' before he could practise it.

Differences:

1. At Qumran an oath is sworn at the beginning of the pre-novitiate, with the Essenes it is the conclusion of the whole novitiate.

2. The Qumran pre-novice was immediately taught *all* statutes (being already bound by oath), while with the Essenes a certain amount of practice and doctrine must have been kept from the novice, since he swore 'to report none of their secrets to others': these 'secrets' could hardly have been imparted to him before the oath.

3. The Qumran novice is admitted to the common meals at stage C, the Essene only one year later, after full membership. This shows that the common meals (the Qumran 'Purity') played a different role in the set-up of each sect.

The Qumran procedure resulted of necessity in the creation of several groups of semi-members: those sworn in but not 'brought near', those living (or having lived) 'within the Community' without partaking in meals, and those partaking in meals but not in drink, who could 'mingle' with the property of the Many, but whose own property was not yet 'mingled'. The Essene procedure, on the contrary, is designed so as to make it easy for the novice to abandon his application until the final stage. It seems to me that the differences, especially the position of the oath, are much more significant than the similarities, although the latter are certainly evidence of a general 'mental climate' in which there was a recognized pattern of novitiate procedure.

We may now proceed to the methods by which the Pharisee

haburah recruited its new members from the ranks of the non-Pharisee or Am-Haareẓ. This is expounded in the Tosephta, Demai, ch. 2.[1] To the first part of this, we have a corresponding Mishnah, Demai 2. 2–3, in which the order is inverted (here given in the order of the Tosephta). For the remainder we can control the Tosephta text from the quotations in P.T. Demai 22d–23a[2] and B.T. Bekh. 30b–31a.

TOSEPHTA DEMAI ii

2. He that imposes upon himself four things is accepted so as to be a haber: that he will not give heave-offering or tithe to an Am-Haareẓ (priest or levite), that he will not prepare his[3] pure food in the house of[4] an Am-Haareẓ, and that he will eat his[5] ordinary food in a state of levitical purity.

MISHNAH DEMAI ii

3. He that imposes upon himself to be a haber sells to an Am-Haareẓ neither wet nor dry produce[6] and does not buy from him any dry produce; he neither stays as guest in the house of an Am-Haareẓ nor does he accept an Am-Haareẓ in his clothes in his own house.[7]

R. Judah says: he also shall not raise sheep and goats, be easy with vows and laughter, contract uncleanness because of contact with a dead person,[8] or minister in a house where a banquet is held.[9] They said to him: these have nothing to do with it.

[1] For which we can now also use Lieberman's edition, i, New York, 1955, and his *Tosephta ki-fĕshuṭah*, i, New York, 1955.

[2] Lieberman, *J.B.L.* lxxi (1952), 199–206, gives for this some variants from the Rome MS.

[3] 'his' om. MS. Vienna (V).

[4] 'with' MS. Erfurt (E).

[5] 'his' om. E.

[6] Wet produce can receive uncleanness, dry produce only if wetted.

[7] Lieberman, *Tos. ki-fĕshuṭah*, p. 209, following R. Jonah, explains the differences between Tosephta and Mishnah by saying that the former deals with conditions to be fulfilled before one can be admitted, the latter with obligations incumbent on the established haber.

[8] If he is a priest, cf. Lev. xxi. 1, 11; M. Bekh. 7. 7.

[9] Reading *beth ha-mishteh* for *beth ha-midhrash*, cf. Epstein, *Mavo lĕ-nosaḥ ha-mishnah*, p. 1210. To understand this, cf. Tos. Demai 3. 6, as quoted in P.T. Demai ii. 23d: 'A haber shall not minister at the banquet or dinner of an Am-Haareẓ unless everything has been properly dealt with and tithed by him personally, including the wine in the carafe. If a haber ministers at such a banquet, people will assume that tithe has been given.' The responsibility is thus on the haber, and 'one must not give anyone to eat things which that person must not eat' (Tos. ibid. 2. 23), thus one is exposed to sinning accidentally.

He that imposes upon himself to be a reliable person (ne'ĕman)[1] tithes what he eats and what he sells and what he buys, and does not stay as guest with an Am-Haareẓ— so R. Meir, but the Sages say: he that stays as guest with an Am-Haareẓ is reliable. R. Meir said to them: such a man is not reliable for himself; can he be reliable for me?[2] Said they: householders never refrain from eating at each others' houses,[3] yet the produce in their own houses is properly tithed.

3. If an Am-Haareẓ has imposed upon himself the obligations of a haber and then becomes suspect with regard to one thing, he is suspect with regard *to all of them—so R. Meir. The Sages say: he is suspect with regard to that thing only.

4. A proselyte[4] who has imposed upon himself the obligations of the Law and then has become suspect with regard to one thing, *even [. . .][5] the whole Law, he is like an apostate Israelite.[6]

5. *If an Am-Haareẓ imposes upon himself the obligations of a haber with the exception of one thing, he is not accepted. (Follows a similar rule about a proselyte, and rules affecting priests and levites.)

9. All these, if they relapse, are never taken back—so R. Meir. R. Judah says: *if they have relapsed openly (παρρησίᾳ), they are taken back, but if they have done

2. He that imposes upon himself to be a reliable person tithes what he eats and what he sells and what he buys, and does not stay as guest with an Am-Haareẓ. R. Judah says: even one who stays as guest with an Am-Haareẓ is reliable. They said to him: such a one is not reliable for himself, how can he be reliable for that which belongs to others?

P.T. AND B.T. (P, B)

*to the whole Law B

*then he is suspect with regard to the entire Law and is . . . B

*If one imposes upon himself to be a reliable person . . . P

*Some transmit it thus: if they did what they did in secret, they are taken back, if openly, they are not B

---

[1] For the reading, see below, pp. 16–17.
[2] The Tosephta printed with the B.T. has: 'can he be reliable with regard to these?'
[3] 'at the houses of other householders who are their friends', P.T.
[4] 'gentile' E, a well-supported reading, cf. Lieberman, Tos. ki-fĕshuṭah, i. 212.
[5] The dots are in E, other MSS. have 'al.
[6] And therefore may marry a Jewess, Lieberman, op. cit., i. 212.

so in secret, they are not taken back.
R. Simeon and R. Joshua b. Karha
say: they are always taken back, for
it is said: Turn, O backsliding
children.[1]

10. *If one who comes to impose
upon himself the obligations of a
haber has previously acted according to them †in private, ‡he is
accepted; otherwise he is first
taught and afterwards accepted.[2]
R. Simeon b. Yohai says: he is in
any case accepted and then taught
as he goes along.[3]

*If we have seen that one B

†in private in his own house B
‡he is accepted and then taught B

11. *And he is accepted[4] first with
regard to wings, and is afterwards
accepted with regard to pure food.
If he only imposes upon himself[6]
the obligations concerning wings,
he is accepted; if he imposes upon
himself the obligations concerning
pure food but not those concerning
wings, he is not considered reliable
with regard to pure food.

* = B; He is made to come closer[5]
with regard to wings and then
taught with regard to pure food P

12. *Until when is a man accepted?
The school of Shammai say: for
fluids thirty days, for clothing
twelve months. The school of Hillel
say: for either †thirty days.

*Until how much B

†twelve months—but this would be
a case in which the school of
Shammai is more lenient than the
school of Hillel! Nay, it is 'either
thirty days' B

13. Everyone who comes[7] *to im-

*to ... himself om. P; + the obliga-

---

[1] This paragraph is quoted B.T. AZ 7ab in a quite different context.

[2] = Tosephta printed with B.T.; Zuckermandel: 'otherwise he is not accepted and afterwards he is accepted'.

[3] 'R. Simeon ... taught' om. E, where wĕ-holĕkhin is drawn to para. 11: 'And
he is accepted progressively'. B.T. adds: 'and he learns in his own way'.

[4] See above, n. 3.

[5] Krotoshin edition maqrivin (but a few lines later the Piel verbal noun qeruv);
Rome MS. mĕqarĕvin. This is, of course, the Qumran term as well as the origin
of the Essene πρόσεισιν, BJ II. viii. 7. Cf. also Akaviah's saying, M. Edu. 5. 7:
'thy deeds will bring thee closer (to Akaviah's "haberim"), thy deeds will make
thee more distant'. Akaviah was associated with Ben Azzai, of the Holy Congregation, see Bacher, Tannaiten, i. 413–14.

[6] 'If he says, I impose upon myself only', V.

[7] Cf. perhaps the Qumran expression 'come into the covenant' for joining the sect?

pose upon himself †must impose upon himself even if he is a pupil-sage, ‡but a sage §who has sat in the meeting (yĕshivah) need not impose upon himself, since he has imposed (these obligations) upon himself from the moment he took his seat; on the contrary, others impose upon themselves before him.

14. *If a person imposes upon himself before a haburah, his sons and slaves need not impose upon themselves †before the haburah, ‡but they should impose the obligations upon themselves before him.

§R. Simeon b. Gamaliel says: if the son of a haber goes wrong, this is not the same as if a haber goes wrong.[1] (Follow rules about the relation between haber and Am-Haareẓ.)

iii. 4. At first they used to say: if a haber becomes a tax-collector, he is deprived of his status as haber.* Later they altered this and said: †as long as he is a tax-collector, he is not considered reliable, once he has withdrawn from being a tax-collector, ‡he is reliable.

tions of a haber B †must impose upon himself before three haberim B ‡but an elder B §who sits B

*Whoever imposes upon himself the obligations of a haber must do so before a haburah, but B †before three B ‡but . . . him om. B; He is answerable (naʿăneh) to the haburah, but his sons and slaves are answerable to him. Some transmit it thus: he and his sons and slaves are answerable to the haburah . . . R. Halaphta b. Saul says: the adults are answerable to the haburah, the minors to him P

§R. Simeon b. Gamaliel says: his sons and slaves must also impose upon themselves before three; if a haber imposes upon himself, it is not as if the son of the haber had imposed upon himself B

*+ if he withdraws from it, he is not taken back B †as long . . . reliable om. BP

‡he is like a haber P; he is like any other person B

The teachers named in connexion with various points of detail

---

[1] Two distinct rules seem to have been confused here, owing to the similarity of *qibbel* and *qilqel*: (a) If a man imposes upon himself before the haburah, his sons, &c., need not do so. R. Simeon says: if a haber accepts the obligations, this does not yet mean that his son has accepted them. (b) After admission, a haber is answerable to the haburah for misdemeanours, his sons, &c., are answerable to him. R. Simeon says: If a haber's minor son does wrong, it is not as bad as if the adult haber does wrong.

are all contemporaries of R. Meir, about A.D. 150. This makes it all the more significant that most of the material is not in the Mishnah. The reason for this, I submit, is that by the time of the final redaction of the Mishnah (*c.* A.D. 200) these rules had lost all practical value; more than that, no one wished to see them restored to practice. Soon all consciousness of the meaning of 'haber' disappeared, and the word was applied to any teacher of the Law—a meaning which, of course, makes nonsense in the context especially of regulations like para. 13.

Büchler[1] claims that these rules were only made in Galilee after 135, and apply only to priests.[2] Throughout his book he insists that we have no means of knowing what a haber is. His anxiety to harmonize the material with 'normal' Jewish practice is perhaps easier to understand if we remember that at his time there existed a school which saw the Essenes everywhere.

We have here three groups:

1. The Am-Haarez. He keeps neither the laws of tithing nor those of levitical purity. He does, however, keep the laws of heave-offering and of the sabbatical year, as also those regarding forbidden meats (and separation of meat and milk?), so that eating at his house is not a sin—P.T. ibid. states that 'an Am-Haarez is not suspect with regard to ritual fitness of food (*kĕsheroth*)'—it is only likely to bring one into the situation of being given untithed food.

2. The reliable person. He keeps the laws of tithing, even if it involves tithing things which may have already been tithed, and avoids the shadow of doubt involved in eating at the house of an Am-Haarez, though he could tithe as he eats.

3. The haber. He observes the laws of tithing, and in addition those of eating in levitical purity, even if he is a layman.

The Tosephta mentions four obligations of the haber, but enumerates only three. Büchler[3] and Lieberman[4] make a slight emendation in the text, by which the fourth condition becomes 'to be a reliable person'. This, however, would make the rest of the

---

[1] pp. 157 seq.
[2] This is above all disproved by the rule about giving heave-offering and tithe.
[3] p. 159.
[4] *Tosepheth Rishonim*, i. 64; *Tosephta ki-fĕshuṭah*, i. 210.

text apply to the haber, so that we should get no information as to what a reliable person has to do. If we accept the version of the Mishnah, and connect the reliable person with tithing, then being a reliable person is still a lower degree, involving as it does an obligation incumbent upon everybody, while the other duties of the haber were supererogatory restrictions accepted voluntarily. It seems the fourth obligation had been forgotten (perhaps, like so many obligations of Qumran members and Essenes, it had something to do with behaviour within the group), and therefore the number was omitted in the more carefully revised Mishnah, which also arranged the two stages in a more logical order and deleted the rules about admission.

Aboth de-Rabbi Nathan, ch. 41, has 'everyone who imposes upon himself four things is accepted as a haber', but enumerates five things: 'who does not go to the cemetery, does not rear sheep and goats, does not give heave and tithe to an Am-Haarez priest, does not prepare his pure food in the house of an Am-Haarez, and eats ordinary food in levitical purity'. These points are gathered from Mishnah and Tosephta, and do not help us.

Both stages, that of a reliable person and that of haber, are entered by means of an action which we have translated 'to impose upon oneself' (*qibbel 'alaw*), and which has to be performed before a haburah, a 'court' of three, or an accredited teacher. That this was a form of declaration closely related to an oath is borne out by M. Bekh. 7. 7, where a priest married to a woman forbidden to him must make a vow not to cohabit with her, and one who has been in the habit of contracting uncleanness from the dead must 'impose upon himself' to discontinue the practice. It is thus a solemn declaration.[1]

The haber makes this declaration before the haburah,[2] apparently in some cases before a court of three (appointed by the haburah?) or even before a single qualified person. Certain classes were—if our information is correct—excused from it, and slaves and minors make their declaration before the master of the house; perhaps in

---

[1] See on this Lieberman, *Tosephta ki-fĕshuṭah*, i. 200.
[2] For *rabbim* = haburah, see Lieberman, op. cit., p. 203; cf. also 'with regard to the Many he is not reliable unless he has imposed upon himself before the Many', Baraitha in P.T. l.c.

the case of minors this was merely a formality[1] and a new declaration had to be made on coming of age. This may be the burden of the statement of Halaphta in para. 14.

As we hear nothing of a separate organization of reliable persons, it is almost certain that also such a person made his declaration before the haburah. Being a reliable person was thus a preparatory stage to becoming a haber, i.e. a novitiate. This is proved by the Tosephta reading in 3. 4: 'once he has withdrawn from being a tax-collector, he is reliable', i.e. just as the Qumran sectarian after a misdemeanour is relegated to the novitiate—provided he repents —the haber, after having removed the cause of the expulsion, becomes 'reliable'. A woman can be reliable though her husband is not (Tos. 3. 9), but apparently cannot be a haber in her own right: 'the wife of a haber is *like* a haber' (B.T. Sheb. 30b; AZ 39a); like a haber's slave, so his daughter and wife remain 'in their status' when passing into the *potestas* of an Am-Haarez, unless they fall foul of haburah practice (Tos. 2. 17); like the slave, the wife, if of non-Pharisee origin, has to 'impose upon herself'—were these the obligations of a haber or of a reliable person? The only argument against considering the reliable person an aspirant for haber status could be brought from para. 5, where according to the Tosephta an Am-Haarez can become a haber straight away. I think we ought to prefer the reading of P.T., allowing him only to become a reliable person, since the Tosephta reading implies that one could become a reliable person without accepting all obligations.

If application for haburah membership had thus to be preceded by being accepted as a reliable person, transition to the status of haber took place in stages. The wording of para. 10 suggests that there were at least three: the formal declaration, a period of study, and admission. The middle stage could be omitted (or shortened?) in the case of persons known to have observed haburah rules before applying. Simeon bar Yohai, in placing the teaching after the formal acceptance and thus turning the haburah into an educational institution, perhaps reflects conditions close to the breakdown of the haburah system.

---

[1] Cf. 'a minor does not require bringing closer', P.T. ibid. This may, however, mean that—as probably at Qumran—children of members were subjected to less stringent tests.

There is, however, another division, of which we have two versions. Para. 11 speaks of acceptance first for 'wings' and then for pure food; para. 12 of acceptance first for fluids and then for clothing.

The meaning of 'wings'—which occurs in connexion with purity laws only here—has not been established.[1] The traditional explanation is that it means 'hands', i.e. the ritual washing of hands.[2] This is supported by P.T. Naz. vi. 10, 55c and by Syr. *kenpē*, 'arms and chest'. S. D. Luzzatto,[3] however, suggested that it means 'clothing', which makes good sense here, and would provide at least one common item for both lists. Indeed, the statement of A. Schwarz,[4] that 'wings' here means the eating of ordinary food in levitical purity, comes to the same; participation in the common meals of the haburah or a meal in a haber's house required, first of all, levitical purity of clothes.

We can obtain larger agreement between the two lists by inverting the order in which the items are mentioned in the opinion of the Shammaites in para. 12. Nothing is said about sequence, and the smaller figure was simply put first.[5] Now both lists name clothing first, the second item being 'pure food' in the first and 'fluids' in the second. The easiest way to account for this difference is to assume that version I deals with the beginning of a stage and version II with the end of the same stage. Even better is the form of version I in P.T. 'he is made to come closer with regard to wings and then taught with regard to pure food': after one year (the Shammaite view in para. 12) he is examined with regard to his punctiliousness in purity of clothing, then, if satisfactory, 'brought closer' and admitted to the common meals, being taught the necessary rules, and at the end of that period admitted to handling fluids (version II).

With reference to the length of these stages, the Hillelite view as given in B.T. agrees with the practice of the Qumran sect. The

---

[1] Cf. the discussion in Büchler, *Der galiläische Amhaarez* (1906), p. 169; Lieberman, *Tosephta ki-fěshuṭah*, i. 215.
[2] Confirmed as a Pharisee law (at any rate for the end of the first century A.D.) by Matt. xv. 2; Mark vii. 2–4; cf., however, Zeitlin, *JQR* xvi (1925–6), 393.
[3] Quoted by Büchler. Cf. the idiom *kěnaf bighdo*.
[4] *Tosifta . . . commentario instructa*, i (1890), f. 52a, n. 79.
[5] Cf. also the inversion of the order in para. 2.

Shammaite view may correspond to a later, easier procedure, in which stage two was shortened. The Hillelite view as given in the Tosephta is probably secondary, made to agree with the correction in B.T.

We may thus set out the stages of admission to the haburah as follows:

A. 'Imposing upon oneself.'
   This leads to the status of 'reliable person', during which one punctiliously carries out the tithing laws.

B. A renewed 'imposing upon oneself' so as to become a haber.
   This leads to a twelve-month period during which one observes the regulations with regard to clothing or 'wings', and is taught.

C. An examination, resulting in 'bringing closer'.
   This admits to being trusted with regard to pure food, i.e. presumably participation in common meals. The period lasts twelve months according to the Hillelites, one month according to the Shammaites.

D. Admission to 'fluids', which constitutes full membership.

Similarities with the Qumran procedure:

1. The oath ceremony comes at the very beginning of the process (against Essene practice).

2. The whole novitiate is divided into three stages.

3. The first stage has a separate name and comports only obligations which properly speaking are incumbent upon every Israelite, not any special Pharisaic regulations, just as the Qumran novice merely 'returns to the Law of Moses', but in the pre-novitiate need not observe the special purity laws.

4. The novitiate is employed as a time of teaching (against Essenes).

5. The novitiate proper is divided into two distinct periods, separated by an examination (against Essenes?).

6. Communion with regard to pure food only comes in the second stage of the novitiate proper (against Essenes).

7. The communion with regard to fluids marks the full admission.

8. No further oath is needed upon full admission (against Essenes).

Differences:

A. The initial oath is taken before a public body, while at Qumran it was taken before the overseer only;[1] apparently it was not, as at Qumran, preceded by an examination.

B. There was a second oath, at the end of the pre-novitiate (different both from Qumran and the Essenes).

As will be easily seen, agreement between the Pharisee procedure and that described in DSD is a good deal closer than between the Qumran sect and the Essenes. At each stage the position of the novice *vis-à-vis* the group is similar, while a member of the Qumran sect would have felt rather uncomfortable in the ranks of Essene novices, not yet bound by oath and not admitted to the common meals. We may therefore say that the initiation procedure forms a strong link between Qumran and the Pharisees, and clearly demands a common organizational origin.

[1] 'stood before the overseer', CDC xv. 11. It should be added that in both cases we cannot be quite sure.

II

PRIVATE PROPERTY IN THE QUMRAN COMMUNITY

THERE can be no doubt that the Essenes practised community of goods.[1] Josephus (*BJ* II. viii. 3) declares that 'it is impossible to find anyone amongst them exceeding others in possessions, for it is a law that those who enter the sect must make their wealth common property (δημεύειν) for the order . . . the possessions of each individual are mingled (ἀναμεμιγμένα) into one, so that they become wealth to all of them as if brothers . . . everyone without difference is obliged to serve for the common good'.[2] In *Ant.* XVIII. i. 5 we learn that 'good men were elected as receivers of income (πρόσοδος) and agricultural produce'. Philo[3] specifies that the members work for others, receiving wages which are used by the elected steward to buy food and other necessities for all.[4] 'None of them would demean himself (ὑπομένει) to acquire any property of his own.' This may be the sense of Pliny's[5] *sine pecunia*. Josephus (loc. cit.) says that they 'despise riches'.

Since the publication of DSD,[6] it seems to have been universally accepted that the Qumran sect had the same system of primitive communism. The idea is mainly based upon the word (*hith*)'*arev* —which recalls so much Josephus' ἀναμεμιγμένα—and the interpretation of *ye*'*anesh*, 'he will be punished'. We shall deal with these two terms later, but must first examine whether other data in the Scrolls support this theory.

[1] Unless one accepts the rather extreme conclusions of Bauer, *P.-W. Suppl.* iv. 403, 410–14.

[2] Reading, with Niese and most MSS., ἀδιαίρετοι. Bekker read αἱρετοι, referring the duty only to the officers.

[3] As quoted in Eusebius, *Praep. Evang.* VIII. xi. 4.

[4] This pooling of outside income for common housekeeping is frequent in modern Palestinian kibbutzim, practised often in combination with economic enterprises of the kibbutz itself. Thus the Essenes may both have carried on their own agriculture and had members working outside.   [5] *Hist. Nat.* v. xvii. 4.

[6] The first to make a detailed comparison appears to have been J. M. Grintz, *Sinai*, xxxii (1952), 11–43.

As far as CDC is concerned, there can be no reasonable doubt that the members of the 'camps' possessed property of their own. They could lose it (ix. 14), it could be stolen (ibid. 11 seq.), they might try to prevent others from enjoying it (xvi. 14–15), and they could quarrel over it (ix. 9–10). These were not merely articles of personal use. A broken passage in xvi. 15 mentions 'his estate' (*ăhuzzatho*), others imply the existence of private threshing-floors and wine-presses (xii. 10), and private possession of farm animals (xii. 9, also xi. 5, 13). There is private buying and selling (xii. 9–11), and members could go into partnership for trade (xiii. 15). They paid only about 8 per cent. of their income ('wages') into a common fund (xiv. 13). The rules about this fund reveal that there were poor men, old men, orphans, unmarried women, &c., requiring assistance. How different from the Essenes where, Philo insists,[1] the sick and old[2] were cared for as in a family. Josephus[3] even speaks of a fund for charity outside the order, including members' relatives. CDC, on the contrary, specifically enjoins members not 'to avert their eyes from' their flesh and blood (vii. 1; viii. 6). While Philo clearly states that the Essenes had no slaves,[4] the sectarians of CDC had slaves, sometimes heathen—i.e. bought from heathen owners—(xii. 10), whom they might urge on to work, except on Sabbath (xi. 12), who lived in their houses, as they did such tasks as carrying children (xi. 11), and whom they could sell (xii. 10).

For these reasons, above all, it has been assumed that CDC represents a different stage in the development of the sect, just as there were non-marrying and marrying Essenes. With regard to the Essenes, however, Josephus specifically says (*BJ* II. viii. 2) that celibacy was a matter of precaution,[5] not of principle; and stresses (ibid. 13) that the marrying Essenes 'are at one with the rest in its mode of life, customs, and regulations'. Any assumption that DSD represented a celibate community should now be dispelled by DSD i*. 4: it is indeed possible that CDC vii. 6 polemicizes against

---

[1] *Quod omnis probus*, 12.
[2] *Praep. evang.* VIII. xi. 13.
[3] *BJ* II. viii. 6.
[4] *Praep. evang.* VIII. xi. 4; Josephus, *Ant.* XVIII. i. 5; *Quod omnis probus*, 79.
[5] One wonders whether this is something corresponding to Rabbinic 'fence regulations'.

some who thought camp life should be celibate, and ought to be translated: 'even though (*wě'im*) they live in camps, according to the custom of the land which existed formerly, they *shall* take wives, according to the disposition of the Law, and *shall* beget children'. The discipline of DSD was not stricter than that of CDC, where in xiv. 20 we have the beginning of a series of punishments corresponding to those in DSD vi. 24–vii. 18. In any event, extensive remains of CDC have been found at Qumran, though we shall know only after their publication whether these include any of the passages quoted above.

It is, however, possible to show from DSD itself that members had private property. vii. 5–8 is preceded and followed by rules about false accusations and 'bearing rancour', and runs:

יתרמה

ואם / ברעהו ונענש שלושה חודשים   ואם בהון היחד יתרמה[1] לאבדו ושלמו
ברושו[2]

ששים יום
ואם לא תשיג ידו לשלמו ונענש

I would suggest reading the verb יתדמה *yithdammeh*, 'keeps silent',[3] and connecting it with CDC ix. 6 where a man is accused of 'rancour' because he keeps silen*t* (*heḥrish*) about another's crime. We would then translate: 'And if he keeps silent concerning his neighbour he shall be punished for three months, but if he keeps silent about (a crime against) the property of the Community, so as to cause it to be lost, he shall himself pay for it, and if he is unable to pay, he shall be punished for sixty days.' It thus becomes more understandable why the crime against the community is punished more lightly: in the case of the individual the crime might, as in CDC, be a capital one.

However, even if we translate the verb, with Brownlee,[4] 'should he have committed an inadvertence against the property of the

---

[1] So the edition of M. Burrows (1951), but see below.

[2] The scribe here left some lines blank, but what follows is clearly the continuation of line 7.

[3] BH has *nidhmah* with a passive or static sense. The Pi'el is conjectural in Hos. iv. 5. The form here (not attested elsewhere) may have been created so as to give a clearly reflexive meaning, and therefore also the *t* was written, against the rule; cf., however, Segal, *Mishn. Hebrew Grammar*, p. 65, n. 2, and the form להנצילם in CDC xiv. 2.

[4] *Manual*, p. 28.

Community', the fact remains that the culprit is expected to pay. Members must thus have had some property apart from the communal possessions, and some more than others, since otherwise the phrase 'if he is unable to pay' makes no sense.[1]

With regard to the 'men of deceit', i.e. the outsiders (ix. 8), the apostate (vii. 24–25), and the sinner during his period of relegation (viii. 23), DSD forbids members to 'mingle' with their property; CDC xx. 7 similarly forbids them to agree (*ye'oth*) with sinners in matters of property and work. This proves that members were able to enter into individual economic relations with outsiders, involving property of their own (*honam*, ix. 8). If we consider the miserable fate of those expelled by the Essenes (*BJ* II. viii. 8 end, quoted below), it must give us to think that men who were expelled from the Qumran sect or relegated to the novitiate for one year could be assumed to possess property and to wish to do business with their erstwhile brethren.

Economic differences are also implied by the rule forbidding one who is insufficiently clad (פוח)[2] to bring out his hand[3] from underneath his garment (DSD vii. 14). This recalls Rabbinic ordinances about people too poor to possess decent garments[4] rather than Philo's statement about the communal supply of clothes among the Essenes.[5] True, Josephus (ibid. 4) says that 'they do not change their garments or shoes until they are torn to shreds or worn threadbare with age', but it is hardly believable that this should have been carried to the extent of violating religious decency, and on top of it punishing people for it.

Indeed, from a hint in CDC we may conclude that one's property played a certain role in fixing one's position within the community. The sectarian transferring from one group to another was examined about 'his actions, his intelligence, his strength, his courage, and his property', and his place in the register fixed accordingly (xiii. 11–12). As we shall see, this may explain the

---

[1] This point has been noted by Gottstein, *VT* iv (1954), 147.
[2] = Mishnaic *poheah*, M. Meg. 4. 6; Targ. *pěhiah* translating *'arom*, Isa. xx. 2–3.
[3] Or 'genitals'.
[4] Büchler, *Der galiläische Amhaarez*, p. 252.
[5] *Praep. evang.* VIII. xi. 12.

registration of the novice's property during the last year of his novitiate.

If the person guilty of damaging, or permitting damage to, communal property is unable to pay for it, he is 'punished' (*ye'anesh*) for sixty days. The same 'punishment' is inflicted for a series of other crimes, both in DSD and in CDC xiv. 20 seq. It is more closely defined in DSD vi. 25: 'they shall set him apart from the Purity of the Many for one year and he shall be punished one fourth of his bread'. Brownlee[1] translates this: 'he shall be fined one fourth of his food allowance'. This has been compared with Josephus' statement about the Essene treatment of heinous sinners (*BJ* II. viii. 8): 'they cast them out of their society . . . as he is bound by the oath he has taken and the customs in which he was engaged, he is not at liberty to partake of such food as he meets with elsewhere, but must eat grass and starve till he perish'. This, however, is no parallel, as the person in question has been expelled from the Essene group altogether, thus gets no food-allowance at all, and in any case his starvation is not engineered by the group, but incidental. At Qumran a member who has been punished for two years 'in the first instance' (DSD. vii. 20) is still well and ready to return. In any case, the culprit is also excluded from the Purity (again in vii. 19)—did the stewards then prepare special unclean meals for those undergoing punishment?

The fact that 'punishment' can be a substitute for payment suggests a more rational and humane explanation: the 'punishment' consisted in a fine paid at regular intervals and fixed at a quarter of the income. With tithes, heave-offering, and the 8 per cent. tax for the poor, this means giving away 45 per cent. of one's income. In the case of damage to communal property this would be a partial repayment at least. I wonder whether the fact that 'sixty days' is written over the line is not significant, and the words should not be deleted. Thus emended, the passage would show that payment went on until full restitution had been made.

Money fines were, of course, well known to Rabbinic law.[2]

---

[1] *Manual*, p. 26.

[2] The list of crimes for which fines were imposed, in the index of S. W. Baron, *The Jewish Community*, iii. 413–14, shows many interesting parallels with DSD.

Sometimes they were fixed in relation to the illegal gain, e.g. one who sold his slave to a non-Jew was fined up to a hundred times the amount gained (B.T. Bekh. 3a). I know of no case where it was related to the culprit's means or payable in instalments. The verb *qanas* (from Latin *census*) also means 'to punish' in other ways, just as *'anash* means among other things a money fine, e.g. Deut. xxii. 18.

This method of punishment, again, implies that members of the Qumran community had a private income which they kept to themselves. The attitude to communal property expressed in the passage we have discussed also shows that the 'property of the Community' was viewed as something completely separate from the property of the members. This is also implied in the statement in the novitiate rules that the first-year novice must not 'mingle' with the communal property, i.e. the second-year novice may do so, although his own property is not yet 'mingled'.

There is still the difficulty of the meaning of *'arev* and *hith'arev*, which are so often applied to property. In Mishnaic Hebrew, the verb does in fact frequently mean 'to mix' and 'to be mixed up'. On the other hand in the Bible, where the verb occurs six times (plus one doublet), it never means 'to be mixed', but in all cases the meaning 'to be in contact with, have business relations with' is the one that fits best. This is clearest in 2 Kings xviii. 23 (= Isa. xxxvi. 8): 'Now, therefore, I pray thee, *hith'arev*[1] with my master, the king of Assyria, and I will give thee two thousand horses if thou be able on thy part to set riders upon them.' It has the same meaning in Prov. xx. 19; xxiv. 21, and also, according to LXX, Pesh., Targ., in Prov. xiv. 16. In xiv. 10 the LXX reading **zadhon* would produce the only certain instance of 'to be mingled', but the reading of MT, &c., 'and in its joy no stranger partakes', is preferable. The meaning 'to have to do with' also fits Ezra ix. 2 and Ps. cvi. 35, where Briggs rightly translates 'have fellowship with'.

In Mishnaic Hebrew the Pi'el mostly means 'to mix' in a physical sense; the Hithpael means physical mixture in M. Yoma 5. 7;

---

[1] All ancient versions translate 'mingle', except Vulg. *transite*, which I cannot explain. A.V. 'give pledges' and R.V. 'make a wager with' go back to Rashi.

M. Middoth 3. 2, while other occurrences in the Mishnah generally mean 'to get mixed up, be confused', not actual physical mixture, cf. especially M. San. 9. 3; M. Zeb., ch. 8. It is difficult to say what meaning lies at the back of *'eruv*, the process by which two Sabbath limits are turned into one, a number of separated properties treated as one for carrying on the Sabbath, or food prepared during a festival preceding a Sabbath identified with that eaten on the Sabbath. Though in all these cases it is a joining rather than mingling, there may have been an idea of symbolic mixture.

The Biblical meaning still exists in M. Kinnim 1. 4, 'if two women bought their pairs of birds jointly (*bĕ-'eruv*)', and Tos. Demai 3. 3, 'In the case of the heave belonging to a haber and an Am-Haarez who have made common cause,[1] one forces the Am-Haarez to take away[2] his share', i.e. to dissolve the partnership.

An *'eruv* is only valid if all those concerned recognize the principle of *'eruv*,[3] i.e. in a purely Pharisee community. Business with an Am-Haarez is hedged around with all kinds of difficulties and precautions, such as retithing or buying victuals at an early, unpollutable stage in their production. 'R. Jonah says: haberim are not open to suspicion that they will either eat or give others to eat (untithed food), R. Yose says: haberim are open to suspicion that they will eat (untithed food), but not that they will give (such food) to others to eat' (Baraitha in P.T. Demai 24a). Indeed, perhaps the most important purpose of the haburah was, within the framework of an agricultural society, to enable its members freely to deal with each other. Even the thing an Am-Haarez has lost may not be publicly announced in a Pharisee synagogue.[4]

That this, business and social contact, was the meaning of the term *hith'arev* in Qumran parlance, clearly results from its use in regulations dealing with non-members and heinous sinners

---

[1] The rendering 'if the heave . . . have become confused' seems to be wrong because this would have made *all* of it unfit for the haber. The joint collection was to the advantage of the Am-Haarez when people hesitated to give heave except to a haber (cf. Büchler, op. cit., p. 93); that is why he has to be *compelled* to take his share.

[2] 'to sell', V and printed editions.

[3] M. Eru. 7. 11.

[4] B.T. Pes. 49b; the same applies to the apostate Jew, Mekhilta on Exod. xxiii. 4.

expelled from the community or temporarily relegated: 'Any man
who . . . and his spirit has become backsliding so as to betray the
Community . . . he shall no more return to the council of the
Community, and no man of the men of the Community shall
"mingle" with him in his Purity or his property' (DSD vii. 24–25);
'Any man of them who transgressed anything of the Law of Moses
high-handedly or underhand shall be sent away from the council
of the Community and shall never return, and no man of the men
of holiness shall "mingle" with his property or his counsel in any
matter' (ibid. viii. 21–24); 'Let their property not "mingle" with
the property of the men of deceit whose ways have not been puri-
fied' (ibid. ix. 8–9).

It is clear that these regulations cannot refer to community of
goods. If the goods of the whole community were held in common,
how could a single individual establish a 'community of goods'
with an outsider? Moreover, how can the property itself—in
the last quotation—establish a community of goods with other
property? The decisive criterion, however, is the addition of
'Purity' and 'counsel' in the first two passages. If 'Purity', as we
have shown, is ritually pure food, and in effect the common meals,
how can the backslider have a 'common meal' of his own? Or
conversely, if 'his' is taken to refer to the sect member, how
can *one* man mingle with an outsider in a group meal? As for
'counsel', mingling makes no sense at all. If we substitute for
'mingle' something like 'make common cause' or 'have contact',
the above sentences become clear and reasonable.[1]

We can even support this translation by a philological proof.
CDC xx. 2–7 reads: 'Every member . . . who was loath to carry out
the commands . . . shall be sent away from the congregation . . .
until the day when he shall stand again in the conclave . . . let no
man agree with him (*ye'oth 'immo*) in property and labour.' The
Niph'al of *'wt* can in no way be taken as 'mingling': since it is used
here in the same manner as *hith'arev* in DSD, we must conclude
that *hith'arev* means the same.[2] Actually it seems that *ye'oth* is

---

[1] 'Making common cause with someone's Purity' means, of course, eating at
his house.
[2] Another synonym is *yiwwaḥedh* (DSD v. 14); but since its meaning is not
clear, it does not help us.

here employed in the Mishnaic sense 'to have enjoyment, benefit from', and is synonymous with the more common root *hnh*, as in *nadhar hăna'ah min*, 'to forswear enjoyment of someone', i.e. to give up all social and economic contact with him.[1] In the same way the sectarian renounces all 'enjoyment' of the property of the non-sectarian or the sinner. The rules in DSD make this very clear: 'and let him not eat or drink anything of their property' (v. 16),[2] which, incidentally, shows that *hon*, 'property', does not always mean money or movable goods. In v. 20 we also get the reason for this: 'all their deeds are uncleanness before Him, and impurity (*tame'*) is in all their property'.

The Qumran sect aimed 'to become a Community in the Law and in property', i.e. to do with regard to their property what they did with regard to the Law—not to share it in equal parts, but to see eye to eye in all matters and be able to trust each other implicitly where the complicated rules of purity, &c., were concerned. During his second year, the novice was not yet permitted to come in contact with the 'property of the Community', because he could not yet be trusted in matters of purity, and thus might convey uncleanness to things concerned with the common meals, or perhaps to the arms stored up for the holy war.

We can now account for the treatment of the novice's property in the rules quoted in Chapter I. The registration of his property by the 'supervisor of the work of the Many' looks at first sight like a preparation for incorporating it into the common fund, but a little thought will show that the opposite is the case. It was registered one year before his final acceptance into the sect; what point could there be in that? Surely the sect did not suspect members of trying to conceal or 'salt away' anything! Indeed, there was no need for registration unless such goods were returnable on leaving. Josephus' description of the fate of those expelled by the Essenes certainly does not suggest that any of their property was returned to them. I would suggest that the property was registered—in the same way as that of the member transferring

---

[1] Cf. M. Ned., chs. 4–5.

[2] Such food taboos are indicated by the Koran, 5. 5: 'The food of those who were brought the book is lawful to you and your food is lawful for them.' This implies that the Muslims did not eat with heathens.

from one group to another (CDC xiii. 11)—for taxation and because of special calls the sect might have to make in emergencies, such as equipping for the final battle, but also in order that the exact extent of landed property might be known for such things as *'eruv*, the fields from which produce could be bought without precautions, &c. The registration was designedly made one year before admission so that the supervisor could keep an eye on the use made of this property, whether it was being properly tithed, whether no *kil'ayim* was grown on it, and so on. He was, however, not allowed 'to bring it out to the Many', i.e. to divulge the information he had received, just as in medieval communities the men who fixed the tax assessments were sworn to secrecy about the information they received about congregants' earnings.

The terminology believed to indicate primitive communism is thus capable of other interpretation, and it seems to me that we must give preference to such interpretation in view of the overwhelming evidence for the existence of private property in CDC. That a high degree of discipline, involving extensive disposal of the group over members' property and finances, does not conflict with the possession of private property by members, or with their integration into a society based on private property, is easily demonstrable from the example of certain contemporary political organizations.

Such a situation certainly does not fit the Essenes, nor any group closely connected with them. There is no 'contempt for riches' here, though on the other hand there is a great deal of social resentment and denunciation of the rich, the exploiters of the poor (DSH xii. 9–10; CDC vi. 16–17, &c.). On the other hand the Pharisee *haburah*, whose methods of recruitment so much resembled those of the Qumran sect, was also an organization with a similar attitude to personal property. Information on these matters is not so complete as on the novitiate procedure, but I believe that a diligent search of Tannaitic material would probably increase the amount of material gathered in the following paragraphs.[1]

[1] Though starting from a different angle, the conclusions of the following paragraphs largely agree with those of Geiger, *Jüdische Zeitschrift*, ii (1863), 25 seq.; cf. *Urschrift und Übersetzungen*, p. 122.

That the haburah exercised disciplinary control over its members
is clear from the regulations collected in Tos. Demai, chs. 2–3.
The haber remained constantly 'answerable' (*na'ăneh*) to the
group. In certain cases he could be expelled and possibly readmitted, much like the Qumran member. Minor misdemeanours
would make a person 'suspect', i.e. presumably cause him to be
closely watched (as the novice was during his time of trial). P.T.
Demai ii. 1, 22c and iii. 4, 23c quote an anonymous saying: 'If a
market stand (σιτοδόκη) was supplied one day with wares pro-
hibited for consumption, that day will be evidence (*hokheah*) for
all other days', i.e. it will—though no immediate action is taken—
count if the same crime is committed again. CDC ix. 16–23 ex-
pounds the system of cumulative conviction, by which punishment is inflicted if the crime has been committed three times
before a number of witnesses insufficient for immediate conviction. The evidence of each witness is written down *bĕ-hokheah*—
an interesting terminological agreement. The form of the word is
peculiar to P.T.[1]

Like the Qumran Community, the haburah collected tithes
for its social services. This was the so-called poor-tithe or second
tithe. A statement in P.T. MSh. v. 9, 56d, in a setting of the
Hasmonean period, gives some interesting additional details: 'At
first the tithe was divided into three parts, one to friends who are
priests or levites, one to the treasury (*ozar*), and one to the poor
and haberim who were in Jerusalem.' Both terms, 'at first' and
'haberim', point to a time when the haburah system still existed.
We thus learn that certain members were maintained by common
funds at the centre,[2] and that there was a central fund, in fact a
'property of the Community'.

Nothing in the context of Tos. Demai suggests that the haburah
held common meals, but we must remember that the word
ḥăvurah can also be employed in a general way for a group holding
a common meal in connexion with some religious occasion, a
ḥăvurah shel miẓwah, e.g. M. San. 8. 2, where as an example is
given the *'ibbur ha-ḥodhesh*, a duty-meal of ten men to mark the

---

[1] See further, Ch. VII, p. 111.
[2] Was this also the economic basis of life at Khirbet Qumran?

new month. Ten is the minimum 'congregation' in Rabbinic law (M. Meg. 4. 3) and at Qumran (CDC xiii. 1; DSD vi. 3). The full formal grace after a meal (*zimmun*) can be pronounced only if ten men are present (M. Meg. loc. cit.); if a priest is present he has the first right to pronounce grace[1] and anyone else who says grace in his presence must say 'by permission of the priest'.[2] 'We have learnt from the school of R. Ishmael: "And thou shalt sanctify him (Lev. xxi. 8)"—for everything connected with holiness: he is the first to begin (at table), the first to say the blessing, and the first to take a choice portion' (B.T. Git. 59b). This corresponds closely to DSD vi. 3–5:[3] 'and together they shall eat and together they shall say the blessing and together they shall take counsel. And in every place where there are ten men of the Council of the Community, let there always be a priest with them, . . . and when they set the table to eat or the must to drink, the priest shall put forth his hand first to obtain a blessing[4] by the first of the bread and the must'. True, the Essenes also gave the priest this prerogative: 'but a priest says grace before meat, and it is unlawful for anyone to taste of the food before grace is said. The same priest, when he has dined, says grace again after meat'. We have here a custom common to all three groups, not a proof of connexion of the Qumran sect with the Essenes. That the custom was archaic in Pharisaic Judaism is shown by the fact that it is handed down in the name of the traditionalist minority school of Ishmael, while the Mishnah (representing here the school of Akiba?) in Git. 5. 8 does not mention the priestly prerogative in meals, but only in reading from the Law at synagogue services, and motivates it by 'avoidance of quarrels' (*darkhē shalom*).[5]

A meal of ten men is a communal effort, and the *ḥăvuroth shel miẕwah* must have met on communal ground or in special buildings.

---

[1] Cf. *Shulḥan 'Arukh*, i. 167. 14; 201. 3.

[2] These words, found in most prayer-books, are missing in Singer.

[3] Cf. also DSD ii*. 17–21.

[4] Read *lĕhibbarekh* (the BH Niph'al, corresponding to MH Hithp.). 'To invoke a blessing upon' (Brownlee) is difficult because of the *bĕ-*. I would suggest that it means that this first bite is a kind of token heave-offering (hence 'the first') which implants a blessing in the rest.

[5] This already amazed Abaye, *c*. 300, cf. B.T. loc. cit. For the position of priests in legal matters, see Ch. VII, p. 98.

In M. Zab. 3. 2 those who eat their food in levitical purity are called *běne ha-kěneseth*: this suggests that such meals were eaten at the *beth ha-kěneseth*, the synagogue.[1] Such cultic associations were of course well known in the Hellenistic east. At Petra, where we have the rock-chambers in which such meals (*mrzḥ*) were held, their members were also designated as *ḥbr*.[2] The classic example of such a meal is the Passover lamb, bought jointly by a number of people, who for the occasion became established as a group, from which it was impossible to withdraw once the lamb had been slaughtered (M. Pes. 8. 3) and which had to keep completely separate while the meal was in progress (ibid. 7. 13). These groups were called *ḥăvuroth*. Geiger, who suggested that the Pharisaic haburah took its origin from the groups around the Passover lamb,[3] quotes three passages implying that ten was the minimum number of participants in one lamb.[4]

With all due reserve, I think that the new evidence of the scrolls gives grounds for reviving Geiger's theory, that the common meals formed an essential part of haburah life and influenced various features of Pharisee practice. It is curious, even against the background of 'life under the Law', that people who were not obliged to do so subjected themselves to the heavy burden of levitical purity in order to eat their food, though Scripture had imposed it only on priests eating heave-offerings. We must distinguish here between sexual purity, which was supposed to be generally observed, and absence of which could impede a divine service (CDC xi. 22), and levitical purity, which in itself had little religious merit. Nor is it natural that priests should attend meals. This was not necessary for their function as instructors (CDC xiii. 2–3). For maintaining levitical purity it was more advantageous to live in separate villages, as seems to have been the actual practice.

The insistence on purity and the presence of priests derive, I would submit, from the idea that the private dinner table is an altar and the meal a form of divine service. This is a well-known

---

[1] The Syr. *ḥabhrūthā dīhūdhāyē*, 'synagogue', suggests that haburah and *kěneseth* may have been interchangeable terms.

[2] Cantineau, *Le Nabatéen*, ii. 93.

[3] *Jüdische Zeitschrift*, ii (1863), 25.

[4] *BJ* vi. ix. 3; Tg. Jer. on Exod. xii. 4; Tos. Pes. 4. 3.

peculiarity of Rabbinic Judaism[1] and may also have been shared by the Essenes.[2] The blessings pronounced before and after the meal correspond to the prayers before and after the sacrifices;[3] it was thus natural to have them pronounced by a priest. However, if priests were to be present, the food, and thus the participants other than priests, had to be kept in a state of levitical purity.

It is significant that the drink consumed at the common meals is called 'must' (tirosh), not 'wine':[4] 'must' is, according to Num. xviii. 12, the form in which the heave is given to the priests. The use of rēshith for the share of the priest makes it very probable that the Numbers passage was in the mind of the author of DSD.[5]

In connexion with this we may note again that levitical purity was not demanded of the 'reliable person'. Yet, while the prohibition of eating in the house of an Am-Haarez sets the reliable person effectively apart from his erstwhile milieu, we hear nothing of a similar separation between the reliable person and the haber, or of a sharper division between haber and Am-Haarez. This makes it probable that in fact the only thing distinguishing the haber from the reliable person was the former's 'dining rights'.

Although eating one's food in levitical purity remained an ideal, and to no small extent influenced medieval Jewish practice, its connexion with the haburah meals was forgotten already in the Amoraic period. It became a sign of outstanding piety, and was attributed to historical personalities like Abraham (B.T. BM 87a) or Saul (Pesiqta Rabb. 68a).[6] It seems also to have been considered a form of divine service or atonement: R. Hiyya the Great sent to his nephew Rab (d. 247) a recommendation to eat his ordinary food in purity throughout the year, or at least during the seven

---

[1] Cf. B.T. Ber. 55a a.fr.

[2] If Quod omnis probus, 75, is taken in the way proposed by Bauer, P.-W. Suppl. iv. 396.

[3] Actually this is not stated anywhere; the Rabbis say that the grace after the meal was introduced by the ancients, cf. B.T. Ber. 48b. They said the same about the three daily prayers, about whose derivation from temple services there can be no reasonable doubt.

[4] DSD vi. 5; ii*. 17–20.

[5] The Rabbinic passages quoted by Grintz, Sinai, xxxii (1952), 15, to show that tirosh is not 'wine', apply to Mishnaic Hebrew, but not necessarily to the Biblicizing language of the scrolls.

[6] See further Büchler, pp. 123–4.

days between New Year and the Day of Atonement (P.T. Shab. i. 5, 3c). As Hiyya came to Palestine in old age (B.T. Suk. 20a), and 'sent' implies a distance, it is possible that this was a Palestinian custom which he had observed.[1]

We have no information about the way in which the haburah system ceased to function, and was replaced by the exercise of Rabbinic authority over the people as a whole. It is *a priori* probable that this happened around the year 70, when the whole fabric of Palestinian Jewish society was altered. There were, however, some curious survivals of the old closed haburah system, with which we shall concern ourselves in the next chapter.

---

[1] The story in B.T. Hul. 107 ab shows that Rab had reservations about the practical possibility of eating in levitical purity, hence he covered his hands with a napkin.

III

THE HOLY CONGREGATION

A group of that name is mentioned in two Amoraic sources:

1. P.T. Ma'aser Sheni ii. 10, 53d:

MISHNAH (2. 9): 'If a man would change a Sela of Second Tithe money in Jerusalem, the School of Shammai say: he must change the whole Sela into small coin; the School of Hillel say: he may take one Shekel's worth of silver and one Shekel's worth of small coin. They that made argument (ha-danim)[1] before the Sages say: three denars' worth of silver and one in small coin.' GEMARA: 'These are they that make argument: Ben Azzai and Ben Zoma. These are the pupils: Haninah ben Hakhiniah[2] and R. Eleazar ben Matthia. The Holy Congregation ('edhah qědhoshah): R. Yose ben ha-Meshullam and R. Simeon ben Menassia.'

The Mishnah recurs in the same form in Edu. 1. 10. 'They that made argument before the Sages' are mentioned once more in B.T. San. 17b, in the context of an enumeration of leading personalities of various schools and groups: 'That make argument before the Sages: Simeon ben Azzai and Simeon ben Zoma and Hanan the Egyptian and Hananiah ben Hakhinai; R. Nahman bar Isaac transmits five names: Simeon, Simeon and Simeon, Hanan and Hananiah.'

The third Simeon, according to Rashi's opinion, is Simeon ha-Temani, mentioned in the same list a few lines earlier: 'At Jamnia there were four: R. Eliezer and R. Joshua and R. Akiba, and Simeon the Temanite was making argument before them on the ground.' This identification is supported by Tos. Ber. 4. 16, where this Simeon is mentioned with Eleazar b. Matthia, Hanina b. Hakhinai, and Simeon b. Azzai as four elders (sic) receiving instruction from R. Akiba.

---

[1] So translated by Canon Danby; see, however, below, p. 45.
[2] The variations of this name are reproduced in the following quotations.

2. Koheleth Rabbathi, ch. 9 (quoted Arukh s.v. *qhl* = A; Yalkut Shimeoni 989 = Y):

'See life with the woman that thou lovest (Eccles. ix. 9). Rabbi (so A; the sons of Rabbi Y) says in the name of the Holy Congregation: acquire a craft together with knowledge of the Law. What is the scriptural basis? "See life, &c.". Why does he (do they AY) call them (it AY) Holy Congregation? Because they were R. Yose ben Meshullam and R. Simeon ben Menassia who(were... who om. AY) used to divide the day into three, a third for study of the Law, a third for prayer, and a third for labour (here ends A). Some say: they toiled in the study of the Law in winter and in labour in summer.[1] R. Isaac ben Eleazar used to call R. Joshua son of R. Timi (call R. Simlai Y)[2] and R. Burqi (Barqai Y) Holy Congregation (here ends Y) because they used to divide the day into three, a third for the study of the Law, a third for prayer, and a third for labour.'

Three further passages mention a group with the Aramaic name *qahălā qaddishā* in Jerusalem:

3. B.T. Ber. 9b: 'R. Yose ben Eliakim[3] testified in the name of the Holy Congregation in Jerusalem: everyone who continues with the 'Amidah prayer immediately after *Ge'ullah* (i.e. the conclusion of the Shema' prayer) will not suffer any harm all that day.'

4. B.T. Beẓah 14b (Yoma 69a; Tamid 27b): 'And behold, R. Simeon ben Pazzi said in the name of R. Joshua b. Levi in the name of R. Yose b. Saul in the name of Rabbi in the name of (*mishshum*) the Holy Congregation in Jerusalem: even if one puts ten sheets on top of each other, and underneath there is one made of wool and linen, one is forbidden to sleep thereon.'

5. B.T. Beẓah 27a (in a discussion as to whether in controversies between R. Judah and R. Simeon the decision is according to the one or the other): 'R. Joseph said: come and hear, for it is attached to mighty tamarisks (i.e. great authorities), for R. Simeon b. Pazzi said in the name of R. Joshua b. Levi in the name of R. Yose b. Saul in the name of Rabbi in the name of the Holy Congregation

---

[1] The words for summer and winter are the Biblical ones, not the MH 'days of sun' and 'days of rains', but this is not unusual in aggadic contexts.

[2] Read, with Hyman, *Tolĕdhoth Tanna'im wa-Amora'im*, p. 635, 'R. Hosha'yah b. Shimi'.

[3] The name occurs only here.

in Jerusalem: R. Simeon and his colleagues made their decision according to R. Meir. Said they (to R. Joseph): but behold, they are much (*ṭūbhā*) older than he! Nay, they decided according to the same principles as R. Meir.'

Rashi's reading was 'R. Simeon b. Menassia and his colleagues'. The Simeon in controversy with R. Judah b. El'ai was, of course, R. Simeon bar Yohai.

6. B.T. Rosh Hashanah 19b: 'R. Joshua b. Levi testified in the name of the Holy Congregation in Jerusalem concerning two Adars, that they are hallowed (officially declared) on the day when the new moon rises.'

A. Hyman[1] thinks that the *qahǎlā qaddishā* is not the same as the *'edhah qĕdhoshah*, while the author of the Arukh (ca. A.D. 1100), by putting references to both in one article, shows that he had a tradition of their identity.[2] The latter is made probable by the presence of Simeon b. Menassia among them, the Amoraic statement (in No. 5) that they were older than R. Meir, and the fact that in Nos. 2, 4, and 5 it is Rabbi who hands traditions down in their name. If they are the same, then it is strange that they should in B.T. constantly occur under an Aramaic name in the context of Hebrew traditions. It might be noted that the traditionists are all Palestinians. Nothing can be concluded from the contents of the various traditions.

The identification of the two groups is supported by a tradition in the Mishnah, which refers to the five 'that make argument before the Sages' of B.T. San. 17b under the title 'elders', as in Tos. Ber. 4. 16 (cf. No. 1):

7. M. Eru. 3. 4: 'R. Yose and R. Simeon say: where there is doubt concerning an *'eruv* it is deemed valid. R. Yose said: Abtolmos testified in the name of five elders concerning an *'eruv* about the validity of which there is doubt.'

The mention together with R. Simeon shows that R. Yose b.

---

[1] Op. cit., p. 1034.

[2] Bacher, *Tannaiten*, ii. 490, n. 2, also thinks they are identical. So do Graetz ('Eine historische Kleinigkeit aus der tannaitischen Epoche', *MGWJ* xix (1870), 33–40) and Hamburger (*Real-Encyclopädie für Bibel und Talmud*, s.v. 'Heilige Gemeinde', Abt. II (1883), pp. 368–9.)

Halaphta is meant, who flourished after 130, so that the chronology fits. The phraseology is that of the *qahălā qaddishā* quotations. The number 'five' also shows that the names quoted in the Sanhedrin list were not just the prominent members of the group, but somehow a fixed body of some authority.

The identification of *qahălā qaddishā* and *'edhah qĕdhoshah* helps us to establish an important fact: that the name 'Holy Congregation' does not belong exclusively to the group Yose b. Meshullam, Simeon b. Menassia, &c., who were contemporaries of Rabbi or later, but was already borne by the group called in No. 1 'they that made argument before the Sages', for the Amoraic remark in No. 5, that they were much older than R. Meir, can only refer to people of the generation of Ben Zoma and Ben Azzai. True, the inference drawn is wrong, for Simeon b. Menassia is younger than R. Meir, and the whole statement belongs to the time of Rabbi, but just because of this the connexion of the Holy Congregation in the mind of the questioner with the earlier group must have been very firm.

By later generations, the Holy Congregation was remembered as a group of—collectively—great halakhic authority, 'great tamarisks', whose traditions Rabbi Judah the Prince was not unwilling to hand down. The curious thing is, however, that their traditions should have been handed down in this collective form and not under the names of the individual teachers, all of whom are recorded in Rabbinic literature as authors of opinions. The most obvious explanation is that the decisions in question were collective—a conclusion also supported by the formula 'Simeon and his colleagues (*hăveraw*)' in No. 5—and formed part of the regulations of the Congregation.

They were, however, not merely a group for study. The name *'edhah* suggests at least a cultic association of some sort, and the addition 'holy' implies that their way of life was such as to deserve such an epithet. The use of this epithet in older Rabbinic usage always refers to strict observation of the Law, and in particular to attention to laws of purity. And indeed the details given in No. 2 imply some form of communal life and suggest that not only were study and prayer performed collectively, but also the work. However little was allowed for sleep, the third of the waking time allotted to work was less than the hours of an oriental labourer, and could only have been realized if the members were their own masters. The second version, distinguishing between summer and winter, makes it probable that the work involved was agricultural.[1]

Neither the insistence on work nor the allotting of a definite part of one's time is unusual in the pattern of Tannaitic Judaism. The distinction of the group is to have brought these requirements into a balanced system which appears to have aroused the admiration of its contemporaries.

What we know of the group is very little, and it is thus all the more remarkable how much of it recalls details from the Qumran writings. This begins with the name. The word *'edhah* is not a common Mishnaic term: all occurrences in the Mishnah are in Biblical quotations and terms. In the Qumran literature it is, on the other hand, the normal word for describing the sectarian organization, the full name of which, probably, was *'ădhath anshe těmim ha-qodhesh*, 'Congregation of Men of Perfect Holiness' (CDC xx. 2), but this is abbreviated in various ways, among which we might mention *anshe ha-qodhesh* (DSD viii. 23), *ish ha-qodhesh* (DSD v. 18), *'ăzath ha-qodhesh* (CDC xx. 24), and finally *'ădhath qodhesh* (DSD v. 20), though the latter possibly may just mean 'a holy congregation', not the name of the sect. Thus the two bodies have to all intents and purposes the same name.

Since the early names mentioned are all connected with Jamnia, the B.T. reference to *qahălā qaddishā dě-birushlem* is remarkable, all the more as it implies the existence of an organization of scholars in Jerusalem after 70, or if it still includes Simeon b. Menassia (No. 5) about 200. The difficulty is, however, not too great. It is fairly certain that during the earlier reign of Hadrian (117–c. 130) there was a small Jewish population in the city[2] and others came there at least during the pilgrimage festivals.[3] Indeed, we find stories involving the presence both of Ben Zoma (Tos. Ber. 7. 5) and of Ben Azzai (M. Yeb. 4. 13) in Jerusalem. It is thus perfectly possible that members of the Holy Congregation met in

---

[1] In Jub. xii. 27 Abraham studies during 'the six rainy months'.

[2] Fullest discussion by Allon, *Tolĕdhoth ha-Yĕhudhim bĕ-Erez Yisra'el bi-thĕqufath ha-Mishnah wĕha-Talmudh*, i. 270–86.

[3] Cf. Baron, *Social and Religious History of the Jews*, 2nd edn., ii. 118.

Jerusalem, perhaps to pray at the ruins of the temple, but also to discuss matters of ritual, and that such decisions were known as those of the 'Holy Congregation in Jerusalem'. The case of Simeon b. Menassia is more difficult: we must, however, take into account the possibility that, although after 134 such meetings were not possible any more, the terminology was kept up.

If indeed this is the explanation for the name, we should have here another parallel to the practice of the Qumran sect, whose legal and ritual rules were established at central conferences called *moshav ha-rabbim*.[1] It seems probable that these took place in connexion with the annual (DSD ii. 19) assemblies and rededication ceremonies described in DSD i–ii.

The division of the day into three parts, study, prayer, and work, was evidently the feature which struck their contemporaries most about the Holy Congregation. We may first of all note the large amount of time given over to prayer, far exceeding that demanded by Jewish ritual and indeed more reminiscent of the exercises of Christian and Muslim devotees. We may, however, compare the 'pious men of old' (*ḥăsidhim ha-rishonim*) who waited an hour before prayer 'that they might direct their heart toward God' (M. Ber. 5. 1). Even more instructive is the version offered as a Baraitha in B.T. Ber. 32b, but apparently as Mishnah in P.T. Ber. 8d: 'the pious men of old used to wait an hour, then pray an hour, and then again wait an hour'. The duty of waiting an hour after prayer is also stated in B.T. loc. cit. by R. Joshua b. Levi, whose connexion with the traditions of the *qahălā qaddishā* is evident from Nos. 4–6, above. The fuller tradition is embedded in a Baraitha, which according to P.T. runs: 'When do they occupy themselves with study and when with their labour? R. Isaac son of R. Eliezer says: because they were pious men both their study and their labour received special blessing.' B.T. has a shorter version lacking the name of this second-generation Palestinian Amora (properly Isaac b. Eleazar or ben Hakula). The enumeration of occupations is the same as with the *'edhah qĕdhoshah*: the B.T. assumes that this adds up to nine hours, but possibly the practice refers only to two prayers,[2] in which case we get a number of hours

---

[1] See Ch. VII, p. 103.   [2] Cf. Allon, *Tarbiẓ*, xi (1939–40), 136–7.

for all prayers roughly corresponding to the third of the waking day. We are not told in what way the 'waiting' time was spent. In passing, it might be noted that the practice here discussed has nothing to do with the Essene devotions before sunrise (Josephus, *BJ* II. viii. 5).

The 'third' allotted to study by the Holy Congregation is logical, but with the Qumran sect we find the 'third' again in connexion with study in DSD vi. 6–8: 'And in a place where there are ten, let there never be lacking a man who interprets the Law continually . . .¹ of each man to his fellow; and as for the Many, let them stay awake in community a third of all nights of the year, to read in the book, and to interpret (*lidhrosh*) the statute, and to pray together.' It is not at all clear whether this means a third of each night (i.e. one 'watch') or one out of every three nights. The first seems more probable on practical grounds.

The idea is not so strange to Rabbinic Judaism as may seem. A Baraitha in B.T. Ber. 4b enjoins: 'when a man comes from his field in the evening, he shall enter the synagogue; if he is trained to read (Scripture) let him read, if he is trained to study the oral law, let him study, then let him recite the Shemaʿ and the ʿAmidah, then eat his meal and say grace, and everyone who transgresses the words of the Sages incurs the death penalty'. The Gemara suggests that the threat refers to those who think that the evening prayer is voluntary, but it is more probably meant to enforce the recommendation of study. Now, according to R. Eliezer's view the last opportunity for saying the Shemaʿ is at the end of the first watch (others place it later) and thus the maximum period of study in the synagogue is one third of the night. As in DSD, too, the period of study is concluded with a communal prayer.

A third of the night is still less than a third of the waking day, but the idea is the same, and the use of the same fraction is suggestive. Since it is not suggested that the Qumran sect and the Holy Congregation are identical, but only that they belong to the same stream, the similarity in terminology weighs heavier than any differences in details of practice, since terminology often tends to survive where practice alters. The 'third' in the case of the

¹ על יפות is still unexplained.

Qumran sect, too, suggests that there was an attempt at balancing study, prayer, and work.

The term for the night study in DSD is *yishqodhu*, 'let them stay awake'. In M. Sot. 9. 15 we learn that 'when Ben Azzai died, the *shaqdanim* came to an end; when Ben Zoma died the *darshanim* came to an end'. In P.T. Ned. viii. 3, 40d, this is quoted by R. Zeira I (Tiberias, beg. of fourth century) in the form: 'Since Ben Azzai and Ben Zoma died (sg.!) the *shaqdanim* have come to an end', but it seems that Ben Zoma's name was added here at a later date.[1] It seems somewhat difficult to take these terms simply as 'eager, industrious'[2] and 'student of Midrash': though respected, these two were by no means the most outstanding scholars of their generation, and Ben Zoma is not a prominent midrashist[3]—if anything, his midrashic utterances are reported with a certain malaise. It should be at least considered whether both these terms are not strictly technical in this context[4] and associate the two with the form of Torah study cultivated both by the Qumran sect and by their own Holy Congregation.

To their particular method of study refers no doubt also the term 'they that make argument before the Sages'. The view that this means they were pupils does not really make sense, since in that case there is no reason why these should be singled out. It is true that none of them bore the title Rabbi: this probably applies also to Hanina (Hananiah) b. Hakhinai, who is so frequently cited without the title that we may suspect it to have been added by copyists in the places where it appears. The reason usually given in the case of Ben Zoma and Ben Azzai is that they died young, before being ordained, but this can hardly apply to Hanina, who was ninety-five years old when killed by the Romans about 130 (cf. *Elleh Ezkerah*, Jellinek's edn., 1853, p. 14). One wonders if the absence of title is not rather due to their failure to seek it, precisely because they derived their authority from their own organization, the

---

[1] In Gen. Rabba 5. 4, both men are called *darshanim* (MS. London: *daroshoth*).

[2] This seems to be the meaning of *shaqudh* (P.T. loc. cit.; Aboth 2. 14).

[3] Cf. Bacher, *Tannaiten*, i. 425.

[4] For *darshan*, cf. the rendering ἐκζήτησις in some Hexaplaric MSS. for *midhrash*, 2 Chron. xiii. 22; xxiv. 27; also Talmudic Aram. *dĕrashā*, 'analogy, legal argument', e.g. B.T. San. 75a.

Holy Congregation.[1] As a mere suggestion, I would like to put forward the view that the curious phrase 'argue before the wise' would in fact fit the type of discussion described in the Qumran scrolls, where certain officials (DSD vi. 12–13)—chosen for their particular expertness in the Law (CDC xiv. 6–10)—ask each member in turn to give his opinion (CDC xiv. 6; DSD vi. 9), speaking out of turn being strictly discouraged (DSD vi. 10; vii. 9, cf., however, vi. 13). All this must have been quite unlike the free discussion in the Rabbinic schools, and well deserved the name of 'making argument in the presence of the Sages', like schoolboys questioned by their teachers.

The Overseer over all the Camps in CDC xiv. 10 is required to have acquired mastery 'in every language according to their families'. It is certainly, to say the least, a remarkable coincidence that the only ones who were said at Jamnia to have had command of 'seventy languages' were precisely the four members of the Holy Congregation: Ben Azzai, Ben Zoma, Ben Hakhinai, and R. Eleazar b. Matthia (P.T. Sheq. v. 1, 48d).[2] The importance of such knowledge can be easily understood in a highly disciplined organization within the multilingual background of Palestinian Jewry (cf., for example, M. Meg. 2. 1), and suggests that the Holy Congregation, like the Qumran sect, was of such a type and of wide extension.

A better understanding of the nature and purposes of the Holy Congregation may be gained by looking a little more closely at those of its members about whom further information is available. It may be useful at this point to draw up a list:

Older Stage (before 130)

Simeon ben Zoma.
Simeon ben Azzai.
Simeon the Temanite.

---

[1] So Büchler, *Der galiläische Amhaarez*, p. 330: 'Der Grund für ihre Zurücksetzung mag ihre Beschäftigung mit der Geheimlehre gewesen sein.' Allon, op. cit., p. 194, thinks ordination depended on character, not on learning alone. In any case, Ben Azzai taught practical halakhah to his 'disciples' (B.T. Ber. 22a), an activity permitted only to ordained Rabbis.

[2] The version in B.T. San. 17b is confused: there is no reference to languages, the four names have been replaced by those of well-known teachers; in this way the end of the tradition, 'if three, &c.', has become unintelligible.

Hanan the Egyptian (otherwise unknown).
Hananiah (Hanina) ben Hakhinai.

Intermediate Stage
(Hananiah b. Hakhinai).
Eleazar ben Matthia.

Later Stage (about 200)
Yose ben (ha-)Meshullam.
Simeon b. Menassia.

Possible Survivals (about 350)
Hosha'yah b. Shammai (Shimi).
Burqi.

Ben Zoma was, of course, a well-known mystic. The few stories told about him show the uneasy attitude of his contemporaries towards him. With a question of interpretation, 'he filled the world with noise' (Gen. Rabba 4. 6); another one of his problems caused R. Joshua b. Hananiah to remark to his disciples: 'Ben Zoma is already[1] outside' (Tos. Hag. 2. 5; P.T. Hag. ii. 1, 77a; B.T. Hag. 15a). Both problems are cosmogonic. It has been pointed out by Scholem[2] that the 'Merkabah' mysticism current among the teachers of the Mishnah and the Talmuds was little concerned with cosmogony. This may explain why Ben Zoma's insistence on cosmogonic problems so much shocked his hearers, who apparently were not particularly scandalized by the extravagances of Merkabah dreamers.

Ben Zoma was not married.[3] He is quoted as saying: 'if you have been put to shame in this world, you will not be put to shame before God in the world to come' (Exod. Rabba 30), a saying reminiscent of Matt. v. 3–5. This is introduced with the words *hayah omer wĕ-dhoresh*, i.e. it is a sample of the activity for which he became famous as a *darshan*. He belonged to the school of R. Johanan b. Zakkai, being a pupil of R. Joshua.[4]

---

[1] *kĕvar* (Tos.; B.T. MSS.); perhaps this means here 'has always been', cf. in P.T. *hărē*, 'behold', and in B.T. MSS. *'ădhayin*, 'still'. In Gen. Rabba 2. 4 'Ben Zoma has gone'.

[2] *Major Trends of Jewish Mysticism*, 2nd edn., p. 73.

[3] Baron, op. cit. ii. 218. I have not been able to trace his source.

[4] Deduced by Hyman from a remark in B.T. Naz. 59b.

Ben Azzai is mentioned, as we shall see below, as Ben Zoma's fellow in mystical studies, but it is stressed that he did not go to the same extremes: 'Hast thou found honey? eat so much as is sufficient for thee (Prov. xxv. 16): that is Ben Azzai; lest thou be filled therewith and vomit it (ibid): that is Ben Zoma' (Midr. Mishle ad loc.[1] He was not married (Tos. Yeb. 8. 4 at end, &c.), or, according to another tradition, he had married or betrothed the daughter of R. Akiba and then separated himself from her for a long period in order to study (B.T . Qid. 63a).[2] Akiba and Ben Azzai lived in the same town, and there was no reason for the separation except the husband's will.

Of Ben Azzai a saying is preserved parallel to that just quoted of Ben Zoma, but in formulation more clearly ascetic: 'If you make yourself despicable for the sake of study, you will in the end be raised thereby' (Gen. Rabba 81. 2; fuller Aboth R. Nathan 11, f. 23b). A curious statement by the two Babylonian Amoraim, Raba (B.T. Eru. 29a) and Abaye (B.T. Qid. 20a), each of whom said of himself, 'I am like Ben Azzai in the streets (*shuqē*) of Tiberias', in the sense of 'I have full authority',[3] suggests that in contrast to other Rabbis he taught in the streets,[4] and that he taught simple people with whom he enjoyed unquestioned authority. His opposition to the usual school set-up seems also to be reflected in 'it would be easier to rule the world than to teach halakhah to people dressed in white cloaks (*sĕdhinim*)' (Aboth R. Nathan 25 end). Dissatisfaction with existing conditions in teaching speaks also from his statement that 'a man must teach his daughter the Law, if only so that she knows not to be afraid if she is innocent and has to drink the bitter waters' (M. Soṭah 3. 4).

Of his Aggadah, 'no kingdom oversteps the limits set to the next kingdom even by a hair's breadth' (B.T. Yoma 38b), links up with the Qumran sect's theory of 'epochs', and the employment of *Gematria* in fixing the date of the Exile (Lam. Rabba on i. 1) not only ranks him amongst those who 'calculate the epochs'

---

[1] In Tos. Hag. 2. 3; P.T. Hag. ii. 1, 77b; and B.T. Hag. 14b the reference to Ben Azzai is lacking.

[2] P.T. Soṭ. i. 2, 16c; B.T. Qid. 63a; cf. B.T. Soṭ. 4b.

[3] Cf. Raba in P.T. Peah vi. 3, 19c: 'I am here the Ben Azzai'.

[4] Cf. also B.T. Ber. 22a: 'Ben Azzai taught it to his pupils in the street'.

(*mĕhashshĕvē qiẓẓin*), but also corresponds to a method employed—probably—in CDC iv. 4–5.

Hananiah b. Hakhinai was introduced to mysticism by R. Akiba, before whom he publicly discussed (?, *hirẓah*) these matters, just as Akiba had done before R. Joshua, and the latter before Johanan b. Zaccai (Tos. Hag. 2. 2, &c.), a tradition significantly enough preserved by the mystically inclined school of Lydda (Judah b. Pazzi). He, too, separated from his wife for twelve or thirteen years while he studied with R. Akiba (B.T. Ket. 62b; Gen. Rabba 17. 3). Of his few preserved teachings, nothing is such as to throw further light upon his personality.

Of Eleazar b. Matthia we know even less (cf. on him Bacher, *Tannaiten*, ii. 374, n. 5, and Büchler, *Amhaarez*, p. 329, n. 3). According to a conjecture by Frankel, *Darkhe ha-Mishnah*, p. 133, he was the son of Matthia b. Heresh, who had lived and taught in Rome.

Even less is known of Simeon the Temanite (cf. Bacher, i. 445–6) and Hanan the Egyptian. If these men really had got their title 'those who make argument before the Sages' from their halakhic prowess, we might have expected to hear a little more of the views which, according to that theory, moved the teachers to set them apart from other students. Also Yose b. Meshullam (Bacher, ii. 489, n. 4) is almost unknown.

A little more is told of Simeon b. Menassia's aggadic statements, though not of his life (cf. Bacher, ii. 489–94).[1] His saying that Israel will not be redeemed until they see the Lord, seek the dynasty of David, and hurry towards the rebuilding of the Temple (Midr. Sam. 13, based on Hos. iii. 5) gives evidence of active Messianism. A distinct ascetic tendency is expressed in his remark on Ps. xliv. 23: 'How is it possible for a man to be killed for God's sake every day? Nay, God reckons it to the pious as if they were being killed every day.' Of occupation with the Law he uses the phrase 'to toil' (Gen. Rabba 63. 1), the same word as in extract No. 2 at the beginning of this chapter for the methods of study practised by the Holy Congregation. His saying that 'the Sabbath

[1] Graetz (op. cit.) has established beyond doubt that he belongs to the time of Judah the Prince.

has been given to you, not you to the Sabbath' (Mekh. on Ex. xxxi. 13)—though the sentiment expressed in it is by no means un-Rabbinic—is formulated in a manner surprisingly similar to Mark ii. 27; cf., however, CDC xi. 16–17 also.

Of particular interest, however, is his application of Dan. xii. 3: 'And they that be wise (ha-maśkilim) shall shine as the brightness of the firmament, and they that turn the many to righteousness (maẓdiqē ha-rabbim) as the stars for ever and ever', in Sifre Deut. 47. After the two groups have been explained as the pious in general and as collectors of charity, Simeon b. Menassia is quoted as saying: 'These are the elders (zĕqenim) . . . who are greater: they who love God or they who cause Him to be loved? . . .' It results that the zĕqenim are teachers; but zĕqenim is precisely the title given to four members of our group who were sitting in the gate-house of R. Joshua (i.e. outside the usual places of learning) and discussing traditions under the guidance of R. Akiba (Tos. Ber. 4. 18);[1] cf. also extract No. 7. It is thus possible that 'elders' is a title held within the organization to which Simeon belonged, the Holy Congregation. In the Qumran sect, the elders were a group next in importance to the priests (DSD vi. 8) and apparently endowed with certain disciplinary powers (CDC ix. 4).[2] The interpretation of the Daniel passage was, as Sifre shows, alien to Rabbinic Judaism, but it is that of the Qumran sect. Maśkil is their term for 'teacher' (e.g. DSD iii. 13); the verb was used for 'to teach' (CDC xiii. 7); in one passage hiẓdiq is used in the same sense (CDC xx. 18).[3]

The Tosephta passage just quoted shows the older group of the Holy Congregation in close contact with R. Akiba, whose pupils

[1] In *Midrash Hallel* (Jellinek's *Beth ha-Midrash*, v. 95) Ben Azzai teaches, Ben Zoma is amongst the taught, and Akiba is not mentioned. The group is called zĕqenim.

[2] *Ant.* xviii. i. 3 states that the Pharisees 'show great respect to those preceding them in years, and will not dare to contradict what these have introduced'. This is close to DSD vi. 26, 'to reject the instruction of his fellow by contradicting his fellow who is written down before him'. This makes one wonder whether Josephus' phrase τοῖς ἡλικίας προήκουσι is not simply *ziqnehem, thus showing that the Pharisee leaders of his time were called zĕqenim. Akiba (Lev. Rabba 11. 8) applied to the Rabbis the term 'elders' only by virtue of comparison with the pentateuchal Elders.

[3] Correct, accordingly, my rendering in *ZD*, p. 40.

Ben Azzai and Hananiah b. Hakhinai are expressly stated to have been. Akiba is again mentioned with the Holy Congregation in a well-known tradition about the four who 'entered the orchard (παράδεισος)' of mystical speculation (Tos. Hag. 2. 3; P.T. Hag. ii. 1; B.T. Hag. 15b); they are Ben Azzai, Ben Zoma, R. Akiba, and Elisha b. Abuya.

R. Akiba, from all we know, produced something like a revolution in Rabbinic studies by his refined methods of discovering scriptural proof for traditional law, which in its final effect largely removed the distinction between the Written and the Oral Law. As R. Tarphon put it on one occasion (Sifra on Lev. i. 5; B.T. Zeb. 13a): 'I have received it as a tradition and cannot explain it: you interpret (doresh) and come to the same result as the tradition.' R. Jonah (c. 350) said: 'Therefore I will divide him a portion among the great (ba-rabbim), and he shall divide spoil with the mighty (Isa. liii. 12)—that is R. Akiba, who has established (hithqin) the interpretation (midrash) of halakhoth and aggadoth'. This, if we pay attention to the wording, can only mean that Akiba applied the same method to halakhah and aggadah. This does not mean, however, that he merely transferred to halakhah processes of thought familiar to his contemporaries from aggadah. While his halakhic innovations seem on the whole to have met with approval, his aggadic efforts came in for sharp reproof, for example by Eleazar b. Azariah, who told him: 'Akiba, what business have you with aggadah, betake yourself to blemishes and overshadowings' (B.T. San. 67b, &c.). Akiba's consciousness of the different nature of his own aggadah is shown by his proud retort to Ishmael: 'For it is not a vain thing for you (Deut. xxxii. 47), and if it is vain for you, this is because you do not know how to interpret (drsh)' (Gen. R. i.).

Akiba's occupation with mysticism is well known. In his partisanship for Bar Kochba he gave proof of his inclination towards active Messianism, as well as the 'reckoning of epochs'.[1] In order to study, he separated from his wife for a period of twice twelve years (B.T. Ket. 62a).

These are traits which appear to link Akiba, too, with the tendencies of the Holy Congregation. In this connexion the curious

---

[1] An example of his technique can be seen in B.T. San. 97b.

fact must be taken into account that certain sayings which are given in Akiba's name appear in other contexts in the name of the 'men of Jerusalem' (cf. Bacher, *Tannaiten*, i. 279). These, as far as I know, are the only traditions given under that heading, and one (B.T. Pes. 113a) is so reported by the same Joshua b. Levi whom we have found as a reporter of sayings of the Holy Congregation in Jerusalem. Bacher (*Tannaiten*, ii. 490) already suspected some confusion here, and it is at any rate possible that the 'men of Jerusalem' is another name for the Holy Congregation in Jerusalem, much as 'men of holiness' is found in the Scrolls (DSD viii. 23) for the 'congregation of holiness'.

On the other hand, it is difficult to imagine that the adherence of a man of such importance should have remained unrecorded in the passages speaking of the Holy Congregation. We may therefore assume that Akiba was on close terms with the Holy Congregation, handed down its maxims, adopted some or all of its exegetic methods, but did not belong to it. Perhaps this is the sense of the conclusion of the story about the four 'who entered the orchard': Akiba 'entered in peace and went out in peace', i.e. he went with the mystics a certain part of the way, but not the whole way.

For it is above all as a society for the cultivation of certain esoteric and ascetic[1] doctrines that we must imagine the Holy Congregation. Here, of course, they again closely resemble the Qumran sect, with its doctrine of the Two Spirits, its belief in Election, its secret writings, and its secret knowledge about the future. The communal life and the formation of a separate halakhah are to some extent by-products of this, but they also belong to the necessary trappings of any close religious society of the period.

We may well ask how it comes that Rabbi Judah the Prince, 'a pronounced rationalist', who 'did all he could to exclude references to the Merkabah, the angelology, &c.',[2] could keep as close a relation to these circles as is shown by extracts 2, 4, 5 above. The

---

[1] On this aspect, see Montgomery, *JBL* li (1932), who stresses the ascetic traits of 'early Pharisaism' (p. 206) and maintains that the N.T. 'shows a reaction against the asceticism manifest in Judaism' (p. 211). We should perhaps add: in the form of Judaism closest to early Christianity, i.e. that of the various pious associations.

[2] Scholem, op. cit., pp. 42–43.

riddle can perhaps be answered to some extent by adducing the example of another outstanding Jewish rationalist, the Gaon Elijah of Vilna (1720–97), who was also a student of Kabbalah. Such relations, however, were possible because, with all the extravagances of a Ben Zoma, the Holy Congregation remained firmly rooted in Rabbinic orthodoxy. Only some members of the circle around Akiba moved farther away, the notable instance being the outstanding halakhic scholar Elisha b. Abuya, who 'cut down the plantations', openly violated Rabbinic enactments, and put the Holy Congregation's maxim, 'acquire a craft together with the study of the Law', into practice by encouraging students of the Rabbinic schools to take up practical trades (P.T. Hag. ii. 1, 77b).

Yet some of the finest sentences about the study of the Law recorded in Rabbinic literature come just from this Elisha (cf. Bacher, *Tannaiten*, i. 434–5). They suggest that his opposition was directed against certain features of second-century halakhic study rather than against the Law itself, perhaps against the creation of a separate group of scholars; cf. also the details given above with reference to Ben Azzai. One wonders whether Bacher (ibid. 436) is right in characterizing him as a man of the world.

As is well known, traditions of Elisha were reported under the form 'others (*ăherim*) say'. It is interesting to note that certain hyper-pietist practices are condemned by the Rabbis as 'another way', *derekh ahereth*, and that two out of these have been identified by S. Lieberman[1] with laws mentioned in the Qumran writings.

It is thus clear that we *need* not go to the Essenes in order to find a parallel to the structure of the Qumran sect, but that there was in Pharisaic-Rabbinic Judaism a tradition which in some respects corresponds better with the Qumran sect than do the Essenes. It therefore becomes essential to base the search for the identity of the Qumran sect upon similarity of practices and doctrines rather than upon organizational features.

[1] *PAAJR* xx (1951), 395–6.

IV

THE SECT AND ITS OPPONENTS

IDENTIFYING the Qumran sect means fitting it into the picture of the religious and socio-political divisions of early Judaism. As none of the names which the sect gives to itself has yet been traced in the sources we possess, two basic attitudes are possible.

Either we can believe the account given by Josephus to be substantially complete, and identify our sect with one of the large schools of thought described by him. If no complete fit can be obtained, we can still select the one where we find the smallest number of definite dissimilarities, assuming that other features observable in the Qumran sect but not found in the existing accounts of the large sects were omitted by those accounts. This is the method of those who have identified the sect with the Essenes.

Or we may assume that Josephus' account is over-simplified and that he omitted a number of groups. In that case we can draw on certain names of groups mentioned by the Talmud or the Church Fathers, such as 'Galilaeans' or 'Dawn Bathers',[1] trying to discover in those names a connexion with what we know of the Qumran sect, or we can try to fit our sect in as a completely new piece in the kaleidoscope.

The second method is really a counsel of despair, and should be adopted only if every attempt to apply the first method can reasonably be said to have failed. The latter can be applied in two directions. One is to find positive agreement—as has generally been done by those who uphold the Essene identification—the other consists in tracing the sect's place by elimination, or in other words, studying the picture it provides of its opponents and identifying the latter. Assuming Josephus' list to be complete, it is then a matter of narrowing down the choice between the remaining groups.

[1] On these, cf. Lieberman, *PAAJR* xx (1951), 395–404.

The picture of the opponents provided in the Scrolls is very full
and complex. It actually distinguishes between different sets of
people:

A. The 'princes of Judah', only in CDC. These men did indeed
'enter a covenant of repentance' (xix. 15), but did not 'depart from
the way of the faithless' (viii. 4); in contrast to the sectarians
who 'departed from the way of the people' (viii. 16), they did not
'withdraw from a people[1] and their sins' (viii. 8; xix. 21). Thus they
have become, quoting the words of Hos. v. 10, 'like them that
remove the landmark' (xix. 15), and God's wrath shall be poured
out over them (ibid.), just as it shall over the congregation of the
Preacher of Falsehood (viii. 13). Amongst their other sins, they
'act overbearingly for the sake of wealth and gain (*beẓa'*)'[2] (viii. 7).
They are also called 'rebels' (viii. 4). It seems fairly obvious that
we have here a group of wealthy men, as opposed to the 'poor'
(DSH xii. 3, 6, &c.) or the 'poor of the flock' (CDC xix. 9) who
make up the sect. Hence, no doubt, they are also the 'princes of . . .
who defraud (*honu*) His holy people' (PPs. 37 ii. 7); perhaps also
'the wicked among the mighty ones' (DST v. 17).

B. 'The builders of the wall' (Ez. xiii. 10), only in CDC. The
wrath of God is kindled against them and He hates them (viii. 18)
and all those that walk after them (xix. 31 seq). They have not
understood the portents of history, because a false teacher has
preached to them (viii. 12). That preacher has also taught them to
sin through 'marrying two women in their lifetime', not 'keeping
separate according to the Law', and marrying their nieces (iv.
19–v. 11).

C. The 'wicked priest', only in DSH. He is a contemporary of
the Teacher of Righteousness and persecuted him personally
(xi. 4–8).[3] He 'was called by the name of truth when he first took
office, but when he had authority over Israel his heart became

---

[1] For a possible emendation, see below, p. 62.

[2] Though in the O.T. *beẓa'* always involves unjust acquisition (except in
mah-bbeẓa', 'what's the use?'), it occurs in CDC x. 18; xi. 15; xii. 7 in contexts
where no such opprobrium is intended; this agrees with Arabic *biḍā'ah*, 'wares',
&c., Eth. *běṣū'*, 'prosperous, happy', where the sense is neutral. Does *hon wa-veẓa'*
perhaps mean '(landed) property and wares'?

[3] If taken in the way of S. Talmon (*Biblica* xxxii (1951), 540–63) and others,
not of Dupont-Sommer. Cf. also PPs. 37 on vs. 32–33 (*JBL* lxxv (1956), 94).

proud' (viii. 8–9). He 'rebelled' (viii. 16),[1] and 'forsook God and was faithless to the laws for the sake of wealth, and gathered in the wealth of men of robbery who had rebelled against the Lord' (viii. 10–11); he 'took unjustly' (ibid.), in particular he 'took unjustly the wealth of the poor in the cities of Judah' (xii. 9–10), he moreover 'took the wealth of gentiles' (viii. 12), just like 'the last priests of Jerusalem who gather wealth and gain from the booty of the nations' (ix. 4–5). He also 'defiled the sanctuary of the Lord' (xii. 8–9). He 'planned to destroy the poor' (xii. 6), and apparently had gone some way towards this aim, since God 'shall repay him according to what he did to the poor' (xii. 2–3).

D. The false teacher. He is called 'the man of lies' (DSH v. 11; CDC xx. 14–15), 'the preacher of lies' (DSH x. 9; CDC viii. 13; PMic. 8. 4), or simply 'the preacher' (CDC iv. 19), the Ẓaw (ibid.), 'he that walks in wind and raises storms and preaches to men with lies' (ibid. xix. 25–26), 'the man of scoffing who dripped (= preached) to Israel waters of falsehood' (CDC i. 14). He is also a personal opponent of the Teacher of Righteousness (DSH v. 11), hence his and the wicked priest's contemporary. He 'despised the Law in the midst of all their [congregation]' (DSH v. 12), and 'misled many . . . for the sake of his glory' (ibid. x. 9–12).

E. The 'expositors of smooth words'[2] (DST ii. 15, 32; PNa. i. 2, 7; cf. CDC i. 18), 'expositors of deceit' (DST ii. 34), 'men of deceit' (DST ii. 16; iv. 20), 'men of scoffing' (CDC xx. 11), 'interpreters of (mĕliẓē) lies' (DST ii. 31; iv. 9–10), 'interpreters of deceit' (DST iv. 7), 'interpreters of error' (DST ii. 14), 'prophets of lies'[3] (DST iv. 16, cf. CDC vi. 1), 'seers of error'[4] (DST iv. 20), 'seers of deceit' (DST iv. 10), 'persuaders to error' (DST iv. 16), 'heralds of sin'[5] (DST v. 36), 'many fishermen who spread out a

---

[1] In the next line the upper part of חוקים, 'laws', is still clearly visible, separated from the verb by one word.

[2] Based upon Isa. xxx. 10, where MT, DSIa, and all versions have 'speak', not drsh. The connexion with Isaiah rules out the rendering 'searchers for'. 'Smooth words' are lies, cf. Prov. vii. 5.

[3] For the Rabbis (M. San. 11. 6) a prophet was a teacher of halakhah, cf. also N.T. προφήτης, 'teacher'.

[4] Also allusion to Isa. xxx. 10; cf. also 'seers of straight things', DST ii. 15.

[5] For kĕruz, 'teaching', see DST vi. 14, as reconstructed by M. Wallenstein, BJRL xxxviii (1955), 247. Cf. also N.T. κῆρυξ, κηρύσσω; and Νῶε δικαιοσύνης κήρυκα = 'teacher of righteousness', 2 Pet. ii. 5. See also p. 98, n. 1.

net and hunt for sons of injustice' (DST v. 8), cf. the nets of false halakhic interpretation spread out by Belial (CDC iv. 15–17).[1] An extensive description of their activity is given in CDC i, stressing firstly their false interpretation and secondly their quarrelsome character. They 'remove the boundary' (CDC i. 16; v. 20), i.e. pervert the traditional interpretations of the Law, against which they speak 'rebellion' (CDC v. 21) or 'error' (ibid. xx. 11) or 'abomination' (ibid. v. 12), claiming that 'they (the laws) are not established' (ibid.); 'they look out for gaps' (ibid. i. 18–19) and 'change Thy Law . . . for smooth words unto Thy people' (DST iv. 10–11), so that in the end they 'justify the wicked and condemn the just' (CDC i. 19). Of their history we learn only that they 'arose in the epoch of the desolation of the land' (CDC v. 20).

There is a certain amount of parallelism between the descriptions applied to the 'princes of Judah' and the wicked priest:

Princes of Judah	Wicked Priest
entered a covenant of repentance	was called by the name of truth
are rebels	rebelled
did not depart from the way of the faithless	was faithless
act overbearingly	his heart became proud
for the sake of wealth and gain	for the sake of wealth
defraud His holy people	took unjustly the wealth of the poor

Between the 'builders of the wall' and the wicked priest only one parallelism can be traced, but that an important one: both he (DSH xii. 8–9) and they (CDC v. 6) are guilty of defiling the sanctuary, hence the 'builders of the wall' were priests.

We may conclude that groups A–C were, if not identical, at any rate closely connected. The wicked priest is the outstanding representative of a patrician and largely priestly wealthy class, who violate the laws in order to indulge their greed or their lust. In particular they oppress the people and the 'poor' economically. Probably it is to them that the epithet *'arizim* is applied,[2] meaning 'ruthless men', or 'oppressors'. It is possible that the 'men of

---

[1] Note that all the attacks against the false teachers appear in the first five columns of DST. This makes one wonder whether the latter part of DST is not an older collection, to which the first columns were added by our sect.

[2] DST i. 39; ii. 11, 21; DSH ii. 6 (‖ *boghĕdhim*); PPs. 37 ii. 12 *'arizē ha[-'am]* ‖ *rish'ē Yiśra'el*; cf. also *'arizē go'im*, PPs. 37 on vs. 14–15, *JBL* lxxv (1956), 95.

robbery' whose wealth the wicked priest gathered were oppressive collectors of priestly dues.

Niece-marriage, as we shall see,[1] was mainly practised in noble and priestly families. Polygamy must have been practically restricted to the wealthier classes; amongst the Rabbis of the Mishnah it seems to have been non-existent. Sexual indulgence, defiling the sanctuary, and oppressive economic behaviour are the crimes of which the Pseudepigrapha constantly accuse the priesthood and the upper classes. The Mishnah has a tradition by which a Sadducee woman is automatically considered to be affected by menstrual uncleanness (Nid. 4. 2),[2] and in B.T. Pes. 57a we have a ditty which gives a graphic picture of oppressive collection of priestly dues:

> Woe to me of the house of Ishmael ben Piakhi,
> woe to me of their fist;
> for they are high priests, their sons treasurers, and their sons-
> in-law temple-trustees,
> and their servants belabour the people with sticks.

Yet there is one important difference between the Sadducee priests of the Pseudepigrapha and the three groups in the Scrolls: the latter had 'entered a covenant of repentance' and 'were called by the name of truth'. They were thus people who had 'taken vows' similar to those of the sect itself—if not actually those of the sect—but had broken their trust. They did 'each man what was right in his eyes' (CDC viii. 8) and 'walked in the ways of the sated one so as to waste away the thirsty one'[3] (DSH xi. 14). However, the 'first members of the covenant' also did 'each man his own desire' (CDC iii. 10–12), and any member of the sect might say: 'nay, I shall walk in the stubbornness of my heart, and his thirsty spirit shall be wasted away with the sated one' (DSD ii. 14). The members of the sect, however, were saved by the intervention of the Teacher of Righteousness (CDC i. 11), through whom God 'revealed to them hidden things concerning which all Israel had gone astray' (CDC iii. 13–14). The Teacher of Righteousness addressed his 'reproof' also to another part of the community, called

---

[1] Below, Ch. VI, p. 91. [2] Cf., however, p. 83.
[3] Deut. xxix. 18; the verse has not been satisfactorily explained, and its exact implication in the Scrolls is not clear.

'the House of Absalom',[1] but they 'were silent' and 'did not help him against the man of lies' (DSH v. 10–11). He no doubt addressed the same reproof also to the 'princes of Judah', the 'builders of the wall', and the wicked priest, but the result was only persecution.

The recalcitrant attitude of these three groups is ascribed to the influence of the 'man of lies' and his group, the 'expositors of smooth words'. He is the one who prevents the 'builders of the wall' from seeing the historical portents, and who does the work of Belial in making his three nets appear to them 'as three kinds of righteousness' (CDC iv. 16–17), and he 'leads (or 'led') the fools into error' (PMic. 10. 4–5). The 'fools' intend to 'keep the Law' (DSH xii. 4–5), as the princes of Judah 'hope for healing' (CDC viii. 4), but the preacher of lies works 'to weary out many[2] by vain service and to cause them to be sated by false actions, so that their labour shall be in vain, forasmuch as they will enter judgements of fire' (DSH x. 11–13). The false teachers are accredited legal authorities to whom the people turn for enlightenment, 'but they withhold the drink of knowledge from the thirsty and for their thirst give them vinegar to drink, so as to look on at their error in behaving foolishly[3] at their festivals' (DST iv. 11–12), 'they cause them to err in a wilderness without a path . . . in order to cause the curses of His covenant to cling to them, to deliver them to the sword avenging the covenant' (CDC i. 15–18).

The false teachers thus err not from ignorance, but intentionally. They are nowhere accused of lust for wealth or carnal pleasures, but the preacher of lies strove 'to build a city of vanity with blood and to establish a congregation with untruth for the sake of his glory'[4] (DSH x. 9–11). The pride of the false teachers may be the meaning of the quotation from Hos. x. 11, 'they chose the fair neck' (CDC i. 19).

These false teachers, with the 'man of lies' at their head, thus form an auxiliary to the wicked priest and the princes of Judah.

---

[1] A Rabbi Absalom *ha-zaqen* is mentioned in Mekh. Ex. xiv. 15 (f. 29b); in other versions אבטולס (Bacher, *Tannaiten*, ii. 550).

[2] Or 'the Many'?

[3] This phrase means wrong halakhic behaviour also in DST ii. 35; iv. 8, 16.

[4] Spelt כבודה, with a suffix form unusual in the scrolls. Yet to read *kĕvuddah*, 'baggage', and to translate it as 'wealth' seems rather far-fetched.

They supply them with the halakhic sanction for their unlawful acts of lust and greed, and at the same time help by misleading the 'fools' and the people.

We know nothing about the opponents of the Essenes. They seem not to have been involved in Hyrcanus' and Jannaeus' persecutions of the Pharisees.[1] Josephus' account rather suggests that they were generally respected and left alone. In any event the picture provided by the Scrolls cannot apply to the opponents of Essenism because of the implication that the opponents were in fact all such as had undertaken to keep the covenant and were in possession of the right laws. It suggests that some priests in authority and serving in the Temple had once been members of the Essene sect, that they and others had defected and become rich, and with the help of false teachers, also from Essene ranks, had succeeded in spreading amongst the people teachings opposed to those (supposedly secret) of the Essenes. This is manifestly absurd, unless the picture Josephus and Philo give of the Essenes is completely wrong, in which case we should have nothing to go on.

We might assume our sect to be Sadducee and the opponents to be Pharisees (the Essenes obviously would be out of question, as they were not 'princes' or priests in high positions). Unless, again, the information of both Josephus and the N.T. is hopelessly wrong, we can hardly imagine the Sadducees in the role of the poor and oppressed. Besides, the statement about the orthodox antecedents of the princes of Judah and the wicked priest implies wholesale defection to the Pharisees.

This last consideration also prevents us from casting the Pharisees in the role of the sect and identifying the opponents as the Sadducees. True, the description of the wicked priest as one who 'was called by the name of truth when he first took office' might apply to some of the Hasmonean high priests, but we can hardly imagine a whole group of 'princes of Judah' to have been first Pharisees and then to have turned Sadducees. The description of the activities of the false teachers, finally, conflicts with Josephus' express statement that Sadducees in public life adopted the practices of the

---

[1] Cf. A. Michel, *Le Maître de la Justice* (1954), p. 223. For Herod's attitude to them, see *Ant.* xv. x. 5.

Pharisees 'because the multitude would not otherwise bear them' (*Ant.* XVIII. i. 4).

There was, however, a change within Pharisaism itself which might have produced the situation described by the scrolls. There can be little doubt that Rabbinic Judaism, as we meet it in Tannaitic literature, is a continuation of Pharisaism,[1] yet it is a curious fact that Rabbinic literature does not openly acknowledge this connexion. The *pĕrushim* are mentioned a number of times, generally with approval, but occasionally with a tinge of enmity.[2] None of the early Rabbis is ever called a Pharisee. Jannaeus[3] 'killed all sages of Israel, the world was desolate until Simeon b. Shetah came and restored the crown to its former state' (B.T. Qid. 66a): not a word about a Pharisee party. Of the early Rabbis Josephus mentions only Pollio the Pharisee and Sameas his disciple (*Ant.* XV. i. 1); if these are Shema'yah and Abtalion of Aboth, ch. 1, they are not called Pharisees there.

To some extent the New Testament supports the idea of a distinction between Rabbis and Pharisees by the frequent mention of 'scribes and Pharisees', once also 'Pharisees and lawyers' (Luke vii. 30) and 'Pharisees and doctors of the Law' (ibid. v. 17). These combinations do not occur in John, except for the non-Johannine viii. 3. In Acts we have only xxiii. 9, 'certain ones of the scribes of the Pharisees' party'. All these show that scribes, &c. (= Rabbis, *sofĕrim*), and Pharisees were not the same thing. On the other hand, we do not get the scribes in such close association with the Sadducees, for whom perhaps Acts iv. 1, 'the priests and the captain of the temple and the Sadducees', is a more significant combination.

There was thus a transition from a stage in which this particular type of Judaism was represented by the 'Pharisees' party' and its institutions to a later stage in which its upholders and official representatives were the Rabbis, with the Pharisaic institutions and party still co-existing for a while. The chief innovation of the

---

[1] I would hesitate, though, to go as far as R. Marcus, that 'Pharisaic Judaism is synonymous with normative Palestinian Judaism of the early rabbinic period (which, of course, was preserved very fully throughout the Middle Ages)' (*Journal of Religion*, xxxii (1952), 154).

[2] M. Soṭah 3. 4; P.T. Ber. ix. 7, 14b.

[3] This is probably the story of Hyrcanus and the Pharisees transferred to Jannaeus.

second stage was that the Rabbis made an attempt to enforce the validity of the Law, as understood in the Pharisee schools, for the whole nation, not only for those who had made a vow to keep it. In other words, they abolished the Am-Haareẓ by taking the Law out of the exclusive keeping of the haburah. The term Am-Haareẓ, indeed, was retained, but gradually gained a new meaning, that of an unlearned person, while the haber became identical with the member of an academy.

The term 'Am-Haareẓ[1] goes back to Neh. x. 27–30, where after the list of signatories we read: 'and all they that had separated themselves (ha-nivdal) from the peoples of the lands unto the law of God . . . every one who knows and studies;[2] cleaving[3] to their brethren, their nobles, and entering into a curse (alah)[4] and an oath to walk in God's law which was given by Moses . . .'. Almost every word in this passage is amply reflected in the Qumran writings. The whole compact is called an ămanah, the term used in CDC xx. 12 of the new covenant at Damascus. The sect frequently uses the Niph'al of bdl to denote the relation between itself and those outside.[5] It will be remembered that Geiger in 1857 suggested that pĕrushim was the Aramaic translation of nivdalim.[6]

It is all the stranger to see what treatment this important passage received in Rabbinic writings. Nowhere within the vast range of Rabbinic literature covered by Hyman's index[7] are these two verses quoted. The list of names which precedes it has become that of the members of the Great Assembly. The compact is not mentioned either by Josephus—though he thinks well of Nehemiah[8]—or by Rabbinic aggadah, which is not so well disposed towards him.[9] There is almost a conspiracy of silence.

The 'peoples of the lands'—'ammē ha-ăraẓoth in this passage and

---

[1] This, of course, is quite different from the pre-exilic Am-Haareẓ, whatever the exact meaning of that term—a representative assembly or the people as a whole.

[2] Cf. CDC viii. 12.

[3] This rendering is probably wrong. In the Scrolls the verb means 'to hold fast (to the Law)', e.g. CDC iii. 12; vii. 13; viii. 2.

[4] In the Scrolls the membership oath is called shĕvu'ah (CDC xv. 6, 8); shĕvu'ath issar (DSD v. 8), while alah is reserved for judicial oaths (CDC ix. 12; xv. 2).

[5] CDC vi. 15; DSD v. 1, 10; viii. 13.   [6] Urschrift und Übersetzungen, p. 103.

[7] Torah ha-kĕthuvah wĕha-mĕsurah, iii. 257.   [8] Ant. XI. v. 6–7.

[9] Cf. Ginzberg, Legends of the Jews, iv. 352; vi. 439.

'*ammē ha-areẓ*, 'peoples of the land', in verse 31—are the heathen living in Palestine. In Pharisaic usage the meaning shifted to the Jewish outsider, and a new singular, '*am ha-areẓ*, was derived from it, denoting a single individual. This shifting of the two concepts 'separation' and 'outsider' from an ethnic-religious to an inner-Jewish field of meaning is characteristic for Pharisaism. It is a semantic development which can only have taken place once and within a closely-knit organization. It is therefore all the more significant that the Qumran sect has the same term. Incidentally, in Qumran parlance the same shift took place in the meaning of 'children of the Pit', which in Jubilees (xv. 26) still means the heathen, but in the Scrolls[1] means Jews outside the sect. The clearest evidence is DST iv. 23–27:

> And Thou didst not cover with shame
> the faces of all those who sought my instruction,
> who gather in Community for Thy covenant . . .
> Thou didst not allow them to be misled by violent men,
> as they planned against them,
> but didst impose their fear upon Thy people
> and make them a hammer for all '*ammē ha-ărazoth*[2]
> to annihilate with judgement all them that transgress Thy command.

The parallelism of 'Thy people' and 'all them that transgress Thy command' excludes the possibility of seeing here a reference to the world conquest of DSW ii. 10 seq. The sense is clearly that the sect will (the whole is no doubt prophetic perfect) be able to impose its conception of the Law upon the outsiders, who at present are unaware of it and do not practise it.

That the outsiders do not practise the Law properly is shown by passages in which the duty of 'withdrawing'[3] (CDC viii. 8) or 'departing' (ibid. 16) from the 'way of the people' (ibid.) is stressed. 'People' is no doubt a convenient short term for 'people of the land', but in viii. 8 we find the curious form *me'am* without the definite article, which looks as if *ha-areẓ* had fallen out after it.[4]

These are probably the 'fools' who are for the time being in the

---

[1] CDC vi. 15 (with *bdl* Niph.); xiii. 14; DSD ix. 16; x. 19; DST ii. 21.
[2] This plural form occurs in Rabbinic literature, e.g. B.T. Shab. 32a.
[3] Niph. of *nzr*, as from unlawful wealth (CDC vi. 15) or whoredom (ibid. vii. 1).
[4] The corruption must have been in the common ancestor of A and B (where *wĕ-ḥaṭṭātham* follows).

clutches of the false teachers, who are 'thirsty' for knowledge, but are given 'vinegar' (DST iv. 11). The fight between the sect and its opponents is thus—in one of its aspects at least—the struggle for the soul of the non-attached part of the people.

This struggle was being carried on, and won, by the group of scholars centred around the Patriarchal house during the second half of the first century A.D. The Talmudic literature is obviously not concerned with telling us the details of this struggle. It does not even reveal to us who was the opponent. From some incidental reports, however, we can see that the battle was to some extent taking place within the Pharisaic-Rabbinic community itself.[1]

At the moment of the fall of Jerusalem the Patriarchal family was in momentary eclipse. The leadership of the movement was in the hands of Johanan ben Zaccai, whose daring action in transferring the centre to Jamnia before the fall of Jerusalem is generally acknowledged to have been the salvation of Rabbinic Judaism. Already before the death of Johanan in 80–85, however, Gamaliel II began to rule, and Johanan with his associates moved to Berur-Hayil. Allon[2] stresses that this can hardly be explained as an act of magnanimity on the part of the old scholar, among whose disciples Gamaliel did not figure.[3] He lists[4] a number of scholars who played an important role under Gamaliel, but were absent from Jamnia in Johanan's time. Some, like Akiba, Ishmael, Tarphon, and Dosa b. Harcinas, might have been too young, but one cannot fail to see some significance in the absence of Nahum of Gimzo, Akiba's teacher, and thereby the founder of the dominant method of interpretation. Still more significant is the absence of certain priestly scholars, some of whom had taught before 70. Two of them, R. Zadok and his son Eleazar,[5] 'we find at Gamaliel's

---

[1] In the next few paragraphs I have largely followed G. Allon, *Tolĕdhoth ha-Yĕhudhim bĕ-Erez Yiśra'el bi-thĕqufath ha-Mishnah wĕha-Talmudh*, i (1952), which through its brilliant use of the sources throws a new light on many matters.

[2] p. 64.

[3] p. 63. The story, told only in B.T., that Johanan asked the emperor to let him take care of 'the dynasty of R. Gamaliel' looks like a late harmonization.

[4] p. 61.

[5] Some deny that Zadok was a priest, cf. Bacher, *Tannaiten*, i. 48, n. 3; cf., on this, Hyman, *Tolĕdhoth Tanna'im wa-Amora'im*, i. 201. Graetz (iii. 485) and Bacher (ibid.) identify him with the Shammaite Zadok of B.T. Yeb. 15b; cf., however, Büchler, p. 120, n. 2.

court in very close contact with him, so to say, as his constant allies',[1] R. Zadok sitting at his right during meetings (P.T. San. i. 4). Their refusal to co-operate with Johanan is perhaps made more understandable if we remember that Johanan forced the priests to pay the Shekel (M. Sheq. 1. 4) and interfered with their right to decide who should be entitled to the financial privileges of the priesthood (M. Edu. 8. 3).[2] Small wonder, then, if of the five outstanding disciples of Johanan (Aboth 2. 8) two, Jose the priest and Simeon b. Nathaneel, have left no traces in Rabbinic literature, Eliezer b. Hyrcanus was put under the ban and all his *ṭohŏroth* were burned,[3] Joshua b. Hananiah underwent painful humiliation at the hands of the Patriarch over a calendar question, with Akiba playing the advocate of administrative authority (M. RSh. 2. 9), and Eleazar b. Arakh withdrew into private life at Emmaus (B.T. Shab. 147b, &c.).[4]

The reason for these differences can hardly be sought in personal ambitions, but there must have been some real and deep points at issue. The instance of the priestly prerogatives gives us a lead. Such an extension of the validity of Pharisaic halakhah to classes of people who had not taken part in its original formation was possible only if it lost some of its rigorism and exclusiveness. In particular it was important to eliminate those regulations which made it impossible for certain classes to be included in the fabric of the community altogether. Thus we learn that older regulations rejected in law-cases the evidence of the Am-Haarez (B.T. Pes. 49b), of 'shepherds, tax-gatherers, and publicans' (B.T. San. 25b), of 'robbers, shepherds, violent men,[5] and all those who are suspect in money matters' (Tos. San. 5. 5). Here we still get the viewpoint of CDC x. 2–3, which rejects as a witness in any type of case[6] him

---

[1] p. 61.

[2] p. 62. We may also mention here that Gamaliel II probably reintroduced the rule that a proselyte must set aside a quarter-Shekel for a bird sacrifice, which Johanan had abolished, cf. Allon, pp. 70–71. The view that Johanan was himself a priest (accepted by Baron, *Social and Religious History*, 2nd edn., ii (1952), p. 117), is refuted by Allon, p. 56. [3] B.T. BM 59b.

[4] In some accounts of Gamaliel's journey to Rome he is accompanied by R. Joshua and R. Eliezer, in others by R. Akiba and R. Eleazar b. Azariah. Allon (p. 77) thinks there were several journeys, and the two first-named took part in the earlier one or ones. [5] *ḥamsanin*, cf. *anshē ḥamas*, DSH viii. 11.

[6] Capital cases having been dealt with in the preceding section.

'who has transgressed anything of the commandment high-handedly'. The Mishnah (San. 3. 3), on the other hand, excludes only 'the gambler, the usurer, pigeon racers, and dealers in produce of the sabbatical year', adding that formerly those who merely stored up agricultural produce in the sabbatical year were also excluded, but the rule was relaxed when this practice became normal owing to the need for meeting Roman tax demands. R. Judah (mid-second century) excluded only those who derived their entire livelihood from these occupations.

In the setting of oriental religious law, being admitted as a witness means that one is considered a full member of the community. The gradual easing of the restrictions therefore indicates that many who were formerly considered outside the pale were now acknowledged as orthodox Jews. Other relaxations of the strict Pharisaic laws, some of which we shall discuss in the following chapters, worked in the same direction. Thus the admission of niece-marriage[1] made it possible for many priests and former Sadducees to hold office in a community from which they would otherwise have been excluded. These relaxations thus had organizational repercussions. They and other, unrecorded, changes led to the fading-out of the old haburah system with its clear distinction between Pharisee and non-Pharisee.

We can well imagine that the haburah did not accept its liquidation lying down. It must have put up a fight for its distinctiveness and privileges. We have no record of that fight, except that we can see its result in the survival of a body like the Holy Congregation. As often in such cases, the struggle led to a polarization in which elements quite unconcerned with the main issue became involved in the ideology of both sides. Above all, the haburah must have fought against those relaxations of the Law which admitted hitherto despised outsiders into the fold, but then the fight easily spread to cover also any other relaxations of legal rigorisms. The polarization was intensified by two other factors. The Patriarchal house collected considerable wealth and associated with the wealthy elements in the community. It developed an ideology of wealth which was in contrast to the simplicity of earlier

[1] See below, p. 92.

Pharisaism: 'God does not cause His Shekinah to dwell except upon one who is strong and rich and wise' (B.T. Ned. 38a); 'R. Simeon b. Menassia said: the qualities which the sages have found in the righteous, namely beauty, strength, riches, honour, wisdom, old age, and many sons, all of these have been fulfilled in Rabbi (Judah the Prince) and his sons' (Tos. San. 11. 8; P.T. San. xi. 4, 30a). As against this, the haburah stressed the simplicity and 'poverty' of its members, although with their fields and slaves they can hardly be called a proletariat.[1] The second decisive policy of the Patriarchal house was its denial of active Messianism. During the Bar Kochba revolt, when Akiba, one of the mainstays of the new school, sided with the Messianists, the Patriarchal court remained pointedly aloof. However, R. Jonathan, a mid-second-century representative of the school of Ishmael, is recorded as the author of the anti-Messianist saying 'may the life-breath go out of them that calculate the epochs' (B.T. San. 97b). 'Calculators of epochs'[2] is a fitting description indeed for the Qumran sect. It will be seen that, although Rabbinic sources give us no inkling of an organized resistance to what we may perhaps call the Rabbinic revolution in Pharisaism, the features to which the Scrolls express opposition are such as befit the first-century Rabbis, and in their totality only them.

Although the present writer is inclined to place the date of the sect after the destruction of Jerusalem, the above considerations apply also to a date in the first half of the first century A.D. I have adduced events of the second half of that century because we know more about it: the social and ideological background of the events which led to the displacement of the Bene Bathyra by Hillel[3]

---

[1] For the social tensions after 70, see S. Klein, '*Bĕ-'iqvoth ha-ărisuth ha-gĕdholah bi-sĕvivoth Lodh*', *Krauss Jubilee Volume*, pp. 69–79.

[2] On the word, see *ZD*, p. 2. CDC mentions five such periods preceding the Messianic age (the 'epoch of Thy glory', DST xii. 22). Prediction of epochs by prophets, DSW xi. 8; 'all epochs of God', DSH vii. 13; 'speeding up' the epochs, DSW i. 12 and Yadin's notes.

[3] Several Bene Bathyra (or Pathora, Tos. Edu. 3. 2) had an academy in Nisibis (B.T. San. 32b); this was already before 70 (B.T. Pes. 3b). In passing, we may mention that Zeitlin (*JQR* xvi (1925–6), 385–6) showed that the 390 years of CDC i. 5 could be calculated so as to make the 'epoch of wrath' begin with the accession of Hillel. The rule for Passover which Hillel introduced is contrary to CDC xi. 17–18, but we are not told that the Bene Bathyra held the view of CDC, only that they did not know. Cf. also p. 90.

and to the victory of the Hillelites over the Shammaites[1] is obscure. Yet it is not impossible that the foundations for the elimination of the haburah system were laid in this period, and that this forms the background of the Qumran opposition. The un-historical approach of Tannaitic and Amoraic literature makes it impossible for us to arrive at definite datings in the earlier Tannaitic period, and there seems little hope of our ever being able to suggest reasonable identifications for the wicked priest and the teacher of falsehood. These persons may in actual fact have been minor scholars delegated to deal with recalcitrant elements, much as the composition of the prayer against the Minim in the Eighteen Benedictions—which must have been a decisive step in driving them out of the synagogues—was entrusted by Gamaliel II to Samuel 'the Small' (B.T. Ber. 28a).

I believe there is a further hint in the scrolls which enables us to fix upon the Rabbis as the opponents of the Qumran sect. One of the outstanding differences between Qumran and Rabbinic literature is the fact that the former is written in Biblical Hebrew, the latter in Mishnaic Hebrew. The 'Copper Scroll', which according to the preliminary announcements so far available[2] is written in 'colloquial Mishnaic Hebrew', shows that this language was not unknown to the dwellers at Qumran; some Mishnaisms in their style and vocabulary prove this quite independently. Their Biblical Hebrew was an idiom artificially and anxiously preserved. We need not go here into the reasons why the Rabbis chose to use the colloquial;[3] they may have done so as part of their policy to give the whole people a share in Judaism as conceived by them, or they may have wished to distinguish their own writings clearly from those of the sectarians. It has been observed by J. N. Epstein[4]

---

[1] Not too much should be made of the greater rigorism of the Shammaite school: though the Qumran sect was also rigorous, every halakhic school was more rigorous than others in some respects. A. Schwarz, *Die Erleichterungen der Schammaiten, &c.* (1893), pp. 14–15, argues that the Hillelites were attempting accommodation with Sadduceeism. Cf. also I. Sonne, *Ginzberg Jubilee Volume* (1946), pp. 275–91.   [2] Cf. *Manchester Guardian* of 30 May 1956.

[3] I follow Noeldeke, Segal, and the present Palestinian school in considering Mishnaic Hebrew to have been a living colloquial. Actually, our argument would still stand if MH were, as most nineteenth-century scholars believed, a Hebrew-Aramaic jargon, as in either case its use would be a concession to the unlearned.

[4] *Mavo lĕ-nosaḥ ha-Mishnah* (1948), p. 1129.

that earlier material in the Mishnah is generally more Biblical in language than later formulations: by extrapolation this points to a stage when the early formulators of Pharisaic-Rabbinic law used Biblicizing language. A change in the language of law can hardly have gone unnoticed: in these matters men are often more conservative than in those affecting the substance. I would suggest that in several passages in the scrolls we have allusions to this change-over:

1. CDC v. 11–12: 'Also they have defiled the spirit of their holy things, and with a tongue of blasphemy (*lĕshon giddufim*) they have opened their mouths[1] against the laws of the covenant.'

2. DST iv. 16–17: 'And they speak to Thy people in a halting language and in another tongue so as to make all their works mad through deceit.'

3. DST ii. 18–19: 'And they have exchanged it (the wisdom of the author) for an uncircumcised language and another tongue for a people of no understanding so as to fail[2] through their confusion (*bĕ-mishgatham*).'

This insistence on 'language' is too remarkable to be dismissed as mere rhetoric. The term 'another tongue' is taken from Isa. xxviii. 11, but the additions are original. In DST ii. 18–19 at least four verses are combined: 'the people that doth not understand shall fail' (Hos. iv. 14), 'for it is a people of no understanding' (Isa. xxvii. 11), 'one of wise mind will accept commandments, but one of foolish language will fail' (Prov. x. 8), 'uncircumcised of lips'[3] (Exod. vi. 12, 30)—all this in order to effect a link between the 'uncircumcised language' and the 'people of no understanding'.[4] The idea seems to be that, just as one 'defiles one's soul' by eating forbidden food (CDC xii. 12), so they defile not only their own holy spirit, but that of the holy things they discuss, by the use of that language.[5]

---

[1] This phrase makes it impossible to take 'tongue' as the organ.

[2] *lĕ-hillavet*, meaning not yet fully explained. In Hos. iv. 14 Tg. translates: 'a people that does not study (*yavin*) will be crushed' (cf. Arab. *labaṭa*, 'throw, trample down'), Aq. and Vulg. 'will be thrashed' (cf. Samar. *labbeṭ*, 'afflict'), Theod. and Rashi 'will be perturbed' (cf. Syr. and MH, and Acc. *lubāṭu*, 'be paralysed').   [3] Said of Moses.

[4] Used CDC v. 16 of the opponents.

[5] Apparently the connecting link is that both food and words pass through the mouth; cf. Matt. xv. 11; Mark vii. 15.

It is intrinsically improbable that this invective is directed against the use of Greek in religious teaching ('uncircumcised language'), nor can we make the Scrolls so late that it would apply to the use of Talmudic Aramaic; in any case, the sect also used Aramaic in its writings. The only other possibility is Mishnaic Hebrew. Its description as a halting language or an uncircumcised (i.e. imperfect or unclean?) language is reminiscent of purists' strictures upon popular languages throughout the ages. More interesting is 'tongue of blasphemy', for if it means what it says, i.e. a language in which blasphemous talk is pronounced in the market place, we should have a valuable contemporary testimony to the colloquial use of Mishnaic Hebrew.

Albeit with some hesitation, I would go farther and explain the unusual *mishgatham* in DST ii. 19 as an ironic allusion to the Mishnah (in the sense of 'study', not yet of the book). Biblical Hebrew attests only *mishgeh* masc. (Gen. xliii. 12), and no occurrence of *mishgah* fem. has been recorded in works accessible to me. This would perhaps not matter so much, were not the root *shagah* in both BH and MH specialized for unintentional transgression, which is certainly not what the author wants to say here.[1] In Qumran parlance oral teaching was designated by the root *hgh*,[2] and *shanah* only occurs in the meaning 'to change' (DST v. 36; xiv. 15). The Rabbis use in *shanah* a term which clearly had not that meaning in BH,[3] where its meaning is represented by the Aramaism *tinnah*; it is significantly only in the later MH of the midrashim that we get *hagah* again in its scholastic sense. Hence it is not impossible that *mishgah* was formed to suggest the sound of *mishnah* and at the same time to imply 'wrongness'.

The Qumran sect, if our argument is correct, were thus a die-hard Pharisee group trying to uphold 'genuine' Pharisaism (as they understood it) against the more flexible ideology introduced by the Rabbis in authority. We can thus expect them to share that

[1] It is a little too involved for the thought of the Scrolls to understand that the sins of the populace were only *shĕghaghah*, 'unintentional sins' (DSD viii. 24; cf. CDC xii. 3–4), because they had been misled. Cf. also 'trespass', p. 101.

[2] Cf. my note, *ZD*, p. 50.

[3] BH has *shanah bĕ-dhavar*, 'to repeat something', but both government and meaning of this word make it improbable that it developed into the MH term, though it may have influenced it and made its borrowing more acceptable.

V

SOME BELIEFS AND PRACTICES

IN any attempt to gain an insight into the theological distinctions between the early Jewish sects, Rabbinic literature is a poor guide. This is due not only to its general unwillingness to be drawn into theological speculation,[1] but even more to the understandable tendency to express tenets of other groups in terms taken from the structure of its own thought. Thus the difference with the Sadducees about free will and predestination is reduced to one about the implications of Antigonos' saying in Aboth 1. 3.[2] The denial of bodily resurrection is nowhere in Rabbinic literature connected with the Sadducees,[3] but even in M. San. 10. 1, where the denial is mentioned without ascription to any definite group, a strong tradition, by adding the words 'provable from the Torah',[4] shows that it was inconceivable that anyone should deny resurrection. In the same context the 'Epicurean' occurs; in P.T. (27d) he is said to be someone who has no respect for the Rabbis.

Josephus is more reliable, both because he lived in a time when there were still Sadducees and because he was interested in theological matters, although he tries to express the differences in terms taken from Greek philosophy. In fact, it is probably due to his familiarity with a system of thought outside Judaism that he

---

[1] Sectarians (Minim) are often given nonsensical replies (e.g. Gen. Rabba 4. 7); this is called 'pushing away with a straw-blade'. It is notable that the sayings of earlier teachers in *Aboth* are of a theological character, the sayings of later ones generally purely ethical.

[2] Aboth de-R. Nathan, ch. 5; cf., on this, Wellhausen, *Pharisäer und Sadduzäer* (1874), p. 46; Schürer, 4th edn., ii. 479.

[3] In B.T. San. 90b, R. Eliezer b. Yose says: 'I proved the forgery of the books of the Minim who say Resurrection is not provable from the Torah.' Some editions have here 'Sadducees' for 'Minim'; in Sifre Num. 15. 31, however, it is 'Samaritans'; cf. on this Geiger, *Urschrift*, pp. 84–86. The words 'ye have forged your Torah' in B.T. clearly point to the Samaritans.

[4] The words are in the ed. princeps, P.T., B.T. (Bomberg 1st edn.; not in some later edns.), and Rashi; but not in the Cambridge, Kaufmann, and Parma MSS., or in Maimonides' Mishnah Commentary.

was able to see and classify the differences within it and, unlike the Rabbis, did not get bogged down in halakhic distinctions.

The main passage is *BJ* II. viii. 14, which states that the Pharisees believed (1) in bodily resurrection, (2) in Divine influence on human actions. To these two distinctions, Acts xxiii. 8 adds (3) that they believed in angels. All three were denied by the Sadducees.

Of these points, (3) is no criterion in reference to the Essenes, who also believed in angels (ibid. 7 end); our sect certainly did.[1] With regard to (2), Josephus (*Ant.* XIII. v. 9) explains that the Pharisees stand in the middle between the Sadducees, believing in absolute free will, and the Essenes, who 'teach that Fate is the absolute master of everything'. The Qumran sect clearly does not side with the Sadducees. Its belief in predestination goes far beyond what we are accustomed to in Rabbinic literature, and at first glance seems to place it with the Essenes. It must be realized, however, that complete predestination really applies only to two classes: the wicked, whom 'God has not chosen from of old, and before they were established He knew their works' (CDC ii. 7–8), and the 'elect', whose names, life-dates, and 'exact statement of their works' are predictable (CDC iv. 4–6). The 'sons of light', however, can 'err' and 'sin', even if it is 'according to the mysteries of God' (DSD iii. 21–23).[2] We are here close to Josephus' actual wording (*BJ* loc. cit.): 'to do right or otherwise rests for the most part with men, but towards each Fate also helps'. On the other hand, this is a region of such fine and gradual distinctions that certainty is impossible, particularly in the absence of any undoubtedly original Essene statement on the matter. Moreover, as the question of predestination is closely bound up with Messianism and with the 'calculation of epochs', it is quite possible that Rabbinic Judaism moved towards a less determinist, Qumran Pharisaism towards a more determinist, position after the separation.

With regard to Essene beliefs about the survival of the soul, Josephus, who was on his own testimony much attracted by this

[1] Cf. in detail Yadin, ch. 9.

[2] Predestination in the Scrolls is most thoroughly discussed by Flusser, *Zion* xix (1953–4), 89–103.

part of their philosophy, is very explicit (*BJ* ii. viii. 11). He leaves no doubt that they believed in an incorporeal survival, not, as did the Pharisees, in bodily resurrection. The position of the Scrolls here is not completely clear. We have a number of passages promising the pious elect that they will live for ever: 'the covenant of God shall stand fast with them to keep them alive[1] for a thousand generations' (CDC vii. 6); 'they are for eternal life' (ibid. iii. 20); 'and they that are according to Thy will shall stand before Thee for ever, and they that go in the way of Thy heart shall be established for eternity' (DST iv. 21–22). These could be construed as expressing the hope that these men—who will live on earth at the Coming—shall never die, since nothing is said about their having been dead.

Three other passages definitely speak of the rising of the dead: 'and then the sword of God shall hasten in the epoch of judgement, and all the sons of His truth shall awake for [   ] wickedness, and all sons of guilt shall be no more' (DST vi. 29–30); 'and they that lie in the dust shall raise a mast, and the worm of the dead ones[2] shall lift up (plural) a standard' (ibid. 34); 'to raise from the dust the worm of the dead ones for a council of [   ]' (ibid. xi. 12). There is a certain amount of similarity with Dan. xii. 2 'and many of them that sleep in the earth of dust shall awake'; yet the literal agreement is curiously lacking: *ye'oru* instead of *yaqizu*; 'that lie' instead of 'that sleep'; 'dust' instead of 'earth of dust'.[3] The difficulty is that the two passages from col. vi stand in a context relating to the Messianic battle. In DSW xii. 4 'the hosts of Thine elect' are represented as fighting along with the angels: Yadin[4] plausibly suggests that these are the pious dead of former generations, and that they fight in heaven against the hosts of Belial. Actually, there is little in the language of DSW against assuming that they fight on earth in a state of resurrection. More weight might be attributed to the passage from col. xi, where the 'council' suggests a resurrection for a longer period.

---

[1] If read as Hiph'il (with *h* omitted), this could mean 'to resurrect them'.

[2] Allusion to Isa. xli. 14, reading with DSIa, Aq., Theod., Vulg. *mēthē Yiśra'el* for MT, DSIb (?), Symm., Pesh. *mēthē Y.* (the variants are not mentioned in Kittel[3]!).

[3] Pesh. 'dust'; LXX, Theod., Vulg. 'dust of the earth'.   [4] Ch. 9, para. 7.

On the basis of the two passages from col. vi Nötscher[1] accepts the sect's belief in resurrection as proven. It might be added that Allegro[2] puts forward an interesting argument for the view that not only the Teacher of Righteousness, but also the wicked priest was expected to be resurrected at the End of Days.

In CDC xx. 10, 13, certain sinners are told that they have 'no share in the house of the Law', which recalls the Rabbinic 'no share in the world-to-come' and the Pauline 'no share in the kingdom of Christ' (or 'of God'),[3] and thus would also speak for belief in the resurrection of the righteous.

Finally, a more direct reference to resurrection may be found in DST viii. 31: 'to destroy (hathem) strength until (the passing of) epochs and to make an end of flesh until set times'. Here, again, the context is far from clear. The preceding lines describe the author's sadness, and in the following line his distress is described in extravagant terms: 'for my strength is made to cease from my body, and my heart is poured away like water, my flesh is melted like wax', &c. This excludes the possibility of referring line 31 to the extermination of mankind, and rather suggests that the poet alludes hyperbolically to his own death. In that case the addition of 'until epochs' and 'until set times' strongly suggests that he thought death to be a temporary state, lasting until the end of the 'epochs' of world history, after which would come the Messianic age and resurrection.

It is very curious, however, that in the various speeches of DSW, the purpose of which is to encourage the warriors to fight unto death, no mention is made of the hope of resurrection. As against this, we must also take note of the fact, to which B. Katz[4] draws attention, that the two 'well-known teachers of the Law', Judas and Matthias, in their inflammatory addresses to the populace (BJ i. xxxiii. 2; Ant. XVII. vi. 2), do not allude even once to resurrection, while on the other hand Josephus himself, in his

---

[1] Zur theologischen Terminologie der Qumran-Texte (1956), p. 151.

[2] JBL lxxv. (1956) 95.

[3] Cf. Koran 3. 176, 'God desires not to give them a share in the world-to-come' (also cf. 4. 53). The Koran has also taken over the Hebrew word as khalāq, though Muslims interpret this as 'luck' (cf. Jeffery, Foreign Vocabulary of the Qur'an, 1938, p. 124).

[4] Pĕrushim, Zĕdhuqim, Qanna'im, Nozĕrim (1947), p. 43.

speech to his comrades at Jotapata (*BJ* III. viii. 5[1]), explicitly refers to it. From this we can hardly, with Katz, draw the conclusion that these teachers of the Law had broken with Pharisee belief, but rather should say that it was not customary to employ the belief in resurrection as a means of moral persuasion.

In ritual, the most outstanding characteristic of Pharisaism is the institution of the three daily prayers, corresponding to the three times of temple sacrifice. For the Essenes, Josephus' statement about their prayer before sunrise (*BJ* II. viii. 5), combined with his silence about prayers in the otherwise detailed description of their day, virtually denies the existence of this institution. We now find in DST xii. 4–6: '. . . and prayer to fall down and to make supplication always from fixed time (*qeṣ*)[2] to fixed time, with the coming of light from [   ] in the seasons of the day according to its fixed order (*tikkun*) of the regular movements (*ḥuqqoth*) of the greater luminary, at the approaching[3] of evening and the going out of the light at the beginning of the dominion of darkness'. These are the three Rabbinic prayer times. The list is followed by a similar enumeration of 'seasons' of the night, and in fact the extensive symbolism and parallelism with historical 'epochs' of the dominion of light and darkness[4] show that the author did not intend to enumerate the times of prayer—all the more significant that he fixed on them in trying to express the idea of continuous prayer.[5] In DSD x. 1–10, where both the festivals and the daily prayer times are used to symbolize continuous worship, the enumeration of the latter (line 10) has become schematized and lost its connexion with ritual practice.

It is possible that we possess a document which proves that our sect even had the Eighteen Benedictions in a form close to the

---

[1] Para. 374 in the Loeb edn.

[2] In this context hardly the historical epoch.

[3] For the interpretation of *lifnoth*, cf. Eth. *fĕnōta*, 'towards', Soqotri *fini*, 'go towards'. The *Minḥah* prayer is properly said between 3 p.m. and nightfall (or, according to another view, 5.45 p.m.), with adjustments for variation in the length of the day.

[4] Cf. DSD iii. 22–23.

[5] 'If one recites the Shema' in the morning and evening, it is as if he had "meditated in His law day and night"' (Midr. Tehillim on Ps. i. 2). Our passage gains in importance if the latter part of DST really is pre-sectarian, cf. p. 56, n. 1.

Rabbinic. This is the hymn inserted in the Hebrew text (not in Greek and Syriac) of Ecclus. ch. li between verses 12 and 13, and which has long been recognized to be a poetical summary (we might almost say a piyyuṭ) of the ʿAmidah Prayer.[1] It contains a benediction which is not in any form of the Rabbinic prayer: 'Give thanks to Him Who hath chosen the sons of Zadok to officiate as priests.' Unless all our ideas about the history of Jewish prayer are wrong, the whole hymn cannot predate the rise of Pharisaism. After the fall of the Temple a Rabbinic author would have had no reason to single out the sons of Zadok rather than the sons of Aaron. We must therefore assume that there were at one time Pharisees who felt so strongly about the legitimacy of the Zadokite priesthood that they inserted this one among the other articles of faith of which the ʿAmidah Prayer consists. We have now two alternatives: either the hymn derives from the Qumran sect or circles close to it, or the benediction for the sons of Zadok existed once in the form used by all Pharisees, in which case the 'Zadokite' attachment of our sect is a feature of Pharisaism in general, and thus provides a further piece of evidence for the Pharisaic character of the sect. It is also interesting to search for a reason why the Rabbis—if this was an old Pharisaic form—should have removed this benediction, and what came in its place. Although by no means all eighteen benedictions of the prayer as we know it are represented in the hymn,[2] it is interesting to point out that it contains no equivalent to the famous *Birkath ha-Minim* (No. XII). Is it possible that the latter took the place of an item which had to be dropped because of its sectarian associations, as was the recital of the Ten Commandments before the Shemaʿ?[3]

If the hymn represents an early form of the ʿAmidah, we must wonder at the presence in it of the fifteenth benediction, in the

---

[1] Really of the whole morning prayer. For 12b cf. Singer's Prayer-Book, p. 17, for 12c p. 100 (evening prayer!), for 12d p. 39, and for 12e p. 44.

[2] The disorder in which they appear in the hymn in its present form suggests the possibility that some lines have been lost. The division of the first benediction into three separate parts also occurs B.T. Pes. 117b.

[3] They were abolished outside the Temple 'because of the noise of the sectarians', B.T. Ber. 12a. However, Elbogen, *Der jüd. Gottesdienst, &c.* (1913), p. 40, explains a passage in P.T. iv. 3, 8a, to mean that before the introduction of XII there were only seventeen. Cf. also Mann, *HUCA* iv (1927), 299.

wording: 'Give ye thanks to Him who causes the horn of the house of David to grow.' Elbogen[1] calls this 'das jüngste Stück der Tefillah'; it is missing in the Palestinian recension from the Genizah,[2] and is mentioned for the first time in Babylonia by Rabba bar Shela, c. A.D. 250 (B.T. Pes. 117b); as Elbogen shows, it is omitted in similar piyyuṭim by the well-known early Palestinian poets. This, however, does not force us to follow Elbogen in assuming that the benediction was invented in Babylonia and that its purpose was to please the Davidic exilarchs.[3] It may well have been an older custom revived in Babylonia;[4] we may imagine the dropping of such a strongly Messianic benediction to have been part of the anti-activist policy of the Palestinian patriarchs, helped perhaps by the fear of Rome and Byzantium.

Before the full publication of the phylacteries from Khirbet Qumran[5] it is too early to discuss the implications of the presence of the Ten Commandments in these, a matter which has some bearing on the relation between the Qumran sect and the Minim of Rabbinic literature.[6]

Of all the ritual peculiarities visible in the Scrolls, the one that sets the Qumran sect most effectively apart from Rabbinic Judaism is thought to be its calendar. The following are the indications of a different calendaric system:

1. Various hints in CDC about the 'correct' manner of celebrating the festivals: 'sabbaths and appointed times' (iii. 14);[7] 'sabbath, appointed days, and the fast-day' (vi. 18–19). The reference may be to the proper method of observance as much as to

---

[1] Op. cit., p. 54; cf. ibid., pp. 39–41.
[2] Ed. Schechter, JQR 1898, pp. 654 seq.; Staerk, Altjüd. liturg. Gebete = Lietzmann's Kleine Texte, lviii (1910), pp. 11 seq.
[3] There is some doubt whether the exilarchate existed before Shapur I (241–72); cf. Baron, Social and Religious History of the Jews, 2nd edn., ii. 195. The late Num. Rabba 18. 21 merely says that XV was introduced later than XII.
[4] Where Rabba bar Bar Ḥana about 300 attempted also to reintroduce the recital of the Ten Commandments (B.T. Ber. 12a); as he had spent much time in Palestine, he may have received the idea from some circles there.
[5] One group of fragments, with the Decalogue, QC I, No. 13, but see the doubts of Gottstein whether this is a phylactery, Kiriath Sefer, xxxi (1955–6), 344. Other phylacteries are said (QC I, 76) to have been found in Cave IV.
[6] Cf. Habermann, Ereẓ-Yiśrael, iii (1953–4), 174 seq.
[7] Also 'to profane the sabbath and the appointed times' (xii. 4).

calendar matters. It may be significant that the list is not, as in Jub. i. 14, vi. 34, 'new moons, sabbaths, and appointed times'.

2. The interference of the wicked priest with the sect's Day of Atonement (DSH xi. 4–8).[1] This most probably shows that they celebrated it on a different day. However, as the story of Gamaliel II and R. Joshua[2] proves, this need not derive from a different calendar system, and may have been so only that year.

3. The explicit statement in CDC xvi. 2–4: 'And the exact statement of the epochs of Israel's blindness to all these, behold it can be learnt[3] in the Book of the Division of Times into their Jubilees and Weeks.' As far as I know, no one has doubted that the book mentioned here is Jubilees, with the Prologue of which the title here shows a remarkable agreement. Moreover, fragments found at Qumran[4] show that the book was read by the sect. The citation does not specify to which particular teaching of Jubilees it alludes: nothing is said about the calendar. There are only one and a half sentences of text before it, dealing with the oath of admission, as does also what follows after our passage. The words immediately preceding are: 'to return to the Law of Moses, for in it everything can be learnt'.[3] Ginzberg and others cut out our passage as a gloss; yet even if it is one, it must come from a sectarian hand: we can hardly imagine a Jew in the Middle Ages to have inserted a reference to Jubilees. Actually, there is no need to cut out the sentence: having recommended the study of the Pentateuch, the author may well have added that Jubilees is a useful commentary on it. It may be true, as Hvidberg[5] remarks, and as seems now to be generally agreed, that this opinion applied especially to the calendaric teachings of that book.

4. The number of priestly watches: twenty-six instead of the Rabbinic twenty-four (DSW ii. 2). Yadin[6] draws from this the conclusion that the sect kept the 364-day year of Jubilees, with exactly fifty-two weeks (12 months of 30 days and four memorial

---

[1] Cf. Talmon, *Biblica*, xxxii (1951), 540–63.
[2] See above, p. 64.
[3] Or 'is set out exactly'.   [4] *QC I*, Nos. 17–18.
[5] *Menigheden af den nye Pagt, &c.* (1928), p. 183.
[6] Ch. 8, para. 3 (4).

days) as against the Rabbinic moon–sun year, which varies between 353 and 385 days, or fifty and fifty-five weeks.

The conclusion is attractive, though not fully compelling. If twenty-four, as seems certain, represents the practice of the last years of the Jerusalem Temple,[1] it was insufficient even in the shortest year for each watch to serve just twice, and in fact the sequence had nothing to do with the calendar. The Qumran sect, by the reform envisaged by Yadin, would thus have made two separate innovations: linking the number of watches with the year, and establishing a year which did not vary. They might, of course, simply have increased the number of classes slightly so as to cater for an average year.[2]

Let us, however, assume that all these are in fact positive indications for the use of the Jubilees–Enoch year of 364 days, with its subdivisions, by the sect.[3] Does this necessarily preclude a common origin for our sect and Rabbinic Judaism? Let us also assume (we have no absolute proof for it)[4] that the Rabbinic calendar was the one kept throughout the Second Temple period, and the other was an innovation. What conclusions can we draw from this?

Jubilees is not the only extra-Biblical book quoted by name in CDC. There is also the 'Book of *Hagi*', quoted three times in CDC and once in DSD i*. 7, and a Testament of Levi (iv. 15).[5] From the fact of citation alone one cannot conclude that the books in question were composed by members of the sect, just as we would not dream of doing so in the case of the Biblical books. It has become fashionable since the discovery of the Qumran literature and the rise of the Essene hypothesis to speak of Jubilees, the

---

[1] The number is given by Chronicles, Josephus (*Ant.* VII. xiv. 7), and Rabbinic sources; see Schürer, ii. 286–9; Yadin, ch. 8, n. 20.

[2] Since 19 Rabbinic years = 19 sun years.

[3] We may see a negative indication in the much-discussed calendar hymn, DSD x. 1–10. Line 3 speaks of luminaries in the plural, and in line 4 we read bĕ-hithḥaddesh⟨am⟩ ziwam (cf. Yadin, ch. 8, n. 26; Burrows: *hem*), 'when their splendour renews itself'; Yadin sees here an allusion to the Messianic light, but it seems to me that it refers to the moon's role in the calendar.

[4] Cf. A. Jaubert, *VT* iii (1953), 250–64, who thinks that the Jubilees calendar is of great antiquity.

[5] On supposed quotations from the Book of Baruch and from a Book of Gehazi, see *ZD*, p. 36.

Testaments, &c., as Essene works, but even if the Qumran sect were Essenes, this does not mean that they read only Essene books any more than the early Christians read only Christian books. If it proves correct that the sect knew Ecclus.,[1] this does not make Ben Sira an Essene, nor does the acquaintance of the Amoraim with a selection of his sayings make him a Pharisee. We can therefore discard from the outset the idea that Jubilees was a book emanating from our sect. Albeck[2] has noted how much farther the halakhah of Jubilees is from the Rabbinic than that of CDC. In some respects CDC halakhah runs counter to that of Jubilees.[3]

If, therefore, Jubilees is quoted as *the* source for the correct calendar, only one interpretation is possible: that the sect got that calendar out of the Book of Jubilees. Note how the citation is introduced: not 'the correct calendar will be found . . .', but 'Jubilees explains how long Israel was ignorant of all this'. This reminds us strongly of CDC i. 9, 'they (the sect) were like the blind and like them that grope their way' until the Teacher of Righteousness came. 'Israel', i.e. the sect, had been 'blind' to the correct calendar, but out of the (ancient) book the truth could be rediscovered.

We may imagine that the following happened: having broken with the central institutions of the Pharisee community, which were now in the hands of their opponents, the sect could no longer make use of the elaborate apparatus which had been created to observe the new moon and report its appearance to the Patriarchal court of law, where witnesses were interrogated by experts.[4] Their own observations, restricted in area, were imperfect and led occasionally to faulty fixations, with the resultant mockery of their opponents. Casting around for a surer guiding principle, they came across Jubilees and accepted its calendar, which in any case suited their almost morbidly systematic mind. We have thus another effect of the polarization after religious schisms mentioned in the last chapter.

---

[1] Cf. Kahle, *VT* i (1951), 46–48.
[2] *Das Buch der Jubiläen und die Halacha* (= 47. *Bericht der Hochschule für die Wissenschaft des Judentums*, 1930), p. 36.   [3] e.g. x. 23; xii. 3.
[4] Actually, according to Allon, *Tolĕdhoth ha-Yĕhudhim, &c.*, i. 67, Gamaliel II already fixed the calendar by calculation.

If this surmise seems too fantastic,[1] we should remember that something of that kind must have happened when the original calendar of Jubilees was invented. We have an instructive parallel in Muhammad's 'reform' of a perfectly good heathen Arabic calendar by removing the institution of intercalary months (*nasi'*) for the sake of consistency.

Once the new calendar had been adopted, the same urge for system may have led the sect to adapt the number of priestly watches to it. It remains strange, though, that in all the polemics of the Scrolls we do not meet any clear reference to the opponents' wrong methods of calculating the calendar. This makes one wonder whether the reference to Jubilees and the twenty-six priestly watches—which, *nota bene*, are to be instituted in the Messianic future—do not indicate that this improved calendar is to be introduced only in the coming Messianic age.

It need hardly be added that we know nothing about the Essene calendar. Josephus' silence appears here rather important: a mathematically perfect time-reckoning of this kind would surely have been grist to his mill, and the different dates for the festivals could hardly have escaped his notice even if he never became a full member of the order.

[1] A remarkable parallel to the development envisaged here existed amongst eleventh-century Karaites in Constantinople—though the solution there was the adoption of the Rabbanite majority's calendar; cf. Z. Ankori, *PAAJR* xxv (1956) 25–38, 157–162.

VI

HALAKHAH

GINZBERG'S demonstration of the Pharisaic character of CDC is principally based upon the halakhic portions (iv. 19–v. 11; ix–xvi), and little can be added to his masterly exposition. DSH adds nothing, DSD only very little which is relevant to this matter. The numerous halakhic details in DSW, which are fully treated in Yadin's edition of that scroll, confirm the conclusions of Ginzberg.

Writers on the Scrolls since 1948 have devoted little space to the halakhic aspect, and seem on the whole to have been left unconvinced by Ginzberg's arguments. The following remarks on this matter, besides attempting to place the problem into a wider background, may perhaps also throw some light on the—mostly unspoken—doubts which caused these writers to bypass it.

Of all ancient systems of Jewish Law, covering both law and ritual, we possess full knowledge only with regard to the Rabbinic one, as formulated between *c.* 100 and 200. Its relation to the Law of the Pharisee sect is a matter of surmise; we shall return to this aspect in the course of the present chapter. In Josephus and Philo we find indications of slightly earlier practice close to the Rabbinic. The exact relation between this and the Rabbinic system has been much discussed and is by no means settled. In the Book of Jubilees, again, a certain amount of ritual is specified. Whether we consider it early Pharisaic or otherwise will of course depend upon our view of the provenience and date of that book.

We are poorly informed about the practice of the Sadducees. Rabbinic literature—both Tannaitic and Amoraic—occasionally mentions Sadducee views. It is not always easy to decide whether these ascriptions are based on a knowledge of Sadducee practice, or are simply the result of a tendency to consider non-acceptable views as Sadducee. Certain statements suggest that the Sadducees were not too insistent upon enforcing their own halakhic views. Josephus (*Ant.* XVIII. i. 4) suggests that in public life the Sadducees of his own time submitted to Pharisee law 'because the multitude would not otherwise bear them'. A story dating from before 70 implies that Sadducee women followed the Rabbis' regulations with regard to menstrual uncleanness (B.T. Nid. 33b).[1]

References to the Essenes touch little on halakhic points proper. The evaluation of Josephus' description is made difficult by our inability to distinguish clearly between points he mentions in order to impress gentile readers with Essene ἐγκράτεια and those by which he wishes to characterize them as different from other Jews. For instance, when he says that they performed prayers just before sunrise (BJ II. viii. 5), this fully agrees with the view of R. Eliezer in M. Ber. 1. 2, with regard to the Shemaʿ; but it is quite likely that the time is only an incidental point, and what he really stresses is the silence before the prayer[2] and the text 'which they have received from their forefathers', i.e. perhaps fixed wording as contrasted with the Pharisaic-Rabbinic practice of leaving the exact formulation to the individual. Again, when stressing that they did not move any implement (σκεῦος) from its place on the Sabbath (ibid. 9), he evidently means to prove by this that they 'are stricter than any other of the Jews', having just mentioned some points (οὐ μόνον) in which 'the other Jews' are also strict; but if what is meant thereby is a form of *muqzeh*[3] regulation (σκεῦος = tool), it is Rabbinic, too. We must therefore assume either that Josephus did not express himself well, and that he referred to something like the later Karaite prohibition of opening chests, &c. (σκεῦος = vessel[4]), or that in his time a less rigorous *muqzeh* legislation was current among his own group.[5] Neither is more than a guess. In any event Essene 'halakhah' is presented in such a way that it can only be understood in comparison with Rabbinic laws.

---

[1] Cf. Tos. Nid. 5. 3 (where the text is less good) and M. Nid. 4. 2; the latter implies that this did not apply to all Sadducee women.

[2] Which is also known from Rabbinic sources; cf. above, p. 42.

[3] i.e. the prohibition of picking up any object the use of which is forbidden on the Sabbath.

[4] CDC xi. 9 forbids opening pitch-sealed vessels on the Sabbath; by implication this means that vessels not sealed with pitch might be opened.

[5] The history of Rabbinic *muqzeh* legislation is one of progressive relaxation; cf. B.T. Shab. 123b.

We know, unfortunately, nothing of the practices of the Judaeo-Christian sects, which no doubt would have been of special significance for our inquiry, considering the striking similarity between the Qumran sect and early Christianity in intellectual climate.

The bulk of the people no doubt did not belong to any of the three parties, but to the Amme-Haarez of Rabbinic literature.[1] As we have seen in Chapter IV, the term was also employed by the sect. These people 'sinned' (CDC xix. 19) and the sect's members were expected to keep away from them; on the other hand, DST iv. 23–27 foresees that in the Messianic time they will be forced to observe the Law correctly, i.e. as it was understood by the sect.

The attitude of the sect towards the Am-Haarez was thus the same as that of the Rabbis: they were held to be ignorant and careless people who did not observe the true laws, though in their heart of hearts they were assumed to acknowledge that these laws were incumbent upon them.[2] All statements about Am-Haarez religious practice are negative. This is a natural point of view for the Rabbis, but we ought to ask ourselves whether the Am-Haarez was really nothing more than an imperfect Pharisee, or whether he was attached to laws of his own, including some positive observances not found in the Pharisee system.

This question is obviously of primary importance in assessing the relation of the Qumran sect to Pharisaism. If all Jews recognized, at least theoretically, the necessity for preserving levitical purity, if the Am-Haarez's failure to wear phylacteries (B.T. Ber. 47b) or to study the Law under the guidance of a teacher (B.T. Sot. 22a) were due to his sloth, then the fact that our sect insisted on these matters simply stamps them as zealous Jews, but does not connect them specifically with the Pharisees, or for that matter with the Essenes. If, on the other hand, the 'popular' Judaism of the Am-Haarez did not recognize these things as binding, then the Qumran sect and the Pharisees belong closely together, and the Essenes, too, must have stood in some genetic relation to these two. The same reasoning would apply to most other agreements between Qumran and

---

[1] Called an 'unclassified centre group' by Marcus, *JBL* lxxiii (1954), 160.

[2] The Mishnah takes the same line with the Sadducees in Nid. 4. 2, where it contrasts Sadducee practice, 'the ways of their fathers', with 'the ways of Israel'.

Rabbinic halakhah, even where we do not specifically learn that the Am-Haarez did not conform.

Since we can be quite certain that Am-Haarez 'halakhah' was never codified, we can only answer our question indirectly. The Samaritans separated from the body of Jewry at a time which lies certainly before the rise of Pharisaism, and the Falashas of Abyssinia in all probability lost contact at an equally early period.[1] Their religious practice and literature are thus likely to throw light upon the pre-Pharisaic common stock of laws. Particularly where the two agree we may equate their practice with that current among the people as a whole. Tannaitic literature supports this to some extent by frequently placing the 'Kuthi', i.e. Samaritan, and the Am-Haarez in the same category. We must of course ignore the references of Babylonian Amoraim to Samaritan haberim (e.g. B.T. Ber. 47b), which are pure theorizing born of unfamiliarity with the true situation and the idea that a haber is simply a learned person. B.T. Nid. 33b even speaks of a Sadducee haber! The underlying assumption is in both cases that Rabbinic law was really acknowledged by both these sects.

Neither Samaritan nor Falasha practice is as fully recorded as one might desire, which is all the more regrettable as in both cases it may soon be too late. The halakhic works of the Samaritans are still largely unedited. For the Falashas, we have a record of Sabbath observance rules in the *Tĕ'ĕzāza Sanbat* (Commandment of the Sabbath) current among them,[2] a composite work of uncertain origin. Its rules show contact with Jubilees, especially with the second list of Sabbath laws in chapter l, but do not seem to be copied from there, as Albeck suggests.[3]

There is, of course, no suggestion that the Qumran sect was close to the Falashas or to the Samaritans, though the latter idea was put forward at one time by K. Kohler.[4] Nor does agreement with

---

[1] For a closer analysis of the place of the Falashas within the general Judaizing of Ethiopian Christianity, see Ullendorff, *J. of Semitic Studies*, i (1956), 216–56.

[2] Translation and commentary in Leslau, *Falasha Anthology* (1951), pp. 3–39, from which the quotations here are taken. In the Introduction, Leslau gives a useful summary of contemporary Falasha practice.

[3] *Das Buch der Jubiläen und die Halacha* (1931), p. 41.

[4] 'Dositheus, the Samaritan Heresiarch', *Amer. J. of Theology*, xv (1911), 404–35.

the marginal sects prove that the sect was not Pharisee, since there may have been a change in Pharisee law, as we shall see in the case of marriage with one's niece. The utilization of these two sources depends on the circumstances, but is sometimes fruitful.

The severity of the Sabbath laws in CDC has been commented upon, and has been taken as evidence for Essene origin. In fact, the rulings in *Tĕ'ĕzāza Sanbat* and Jubilees are much more rigid; the same applies to the Samaritan Sabbath. Compared with these, CDC is lenient: while it adds nothing new, it closely approaches Rabbinic halakhah.[1] In particular, it actually polemicizes against the imposition of the death-penalty for Sabbath-breaking (xii. 4–6), which is Biblical (Num. xv. 35), and emphatically enjoined by Jubilees and T.S., and is admitted by M. San. 7. 4, 8; B.T. Yeb. 47a. On the whole, the rules in CDC lie in a direct line of development from the earlier, severe practice to that of the Rabbis.

Since amongst all the Rabbinic complaints about the Am-Haarez it is never said that he does not observe the Sabbath, he no doubt kept that day as he had inherited it from his forefathers. The insistence of the Rabbis (Tos. Shab. 15. 11–16; B.T. Yoma 84b) and CDC (xi. 16–17) on the permissibility of *all* means to save a life on the Sabbath strongly suggests that the ordinary man hesitated to do so. The strict observance was thus by no means introduced by the Pharisees. In fact, a story preserved in several places[2] relates that 'in the days of the Greeks'[3] a man was executed for riding a horse on the Sabbath, by Rabbinic standards not a punishable transgression, but punished with death by T.S. and Jubilees.[4] Eliezer b. Jacob (probably the first-generation Tanna) who reports this could only explain it as an emergency measure. It is interesting that Jubilees agrees here, both in general and in particular, with the pre-Pharisee halakhah. The progress towards leniency must thus have taken place *within* Pharisaism, and agreement in details between the Qumran sect and Rabbinic law is of primary significance.

As the archaeological evidence now rules out any identification of our sect with the Karaites, in the sense of the movement which began in the eighth century A.D., comparison of its halakhah with

---

[1] For details, see *ZD*, pp. 52–58.
[2] P.T. Ḥag. ii. 1, 77a; B.T. Yeb. 90b; B.T. San. 46a.
[3] Not in the P.T. version.   [4] Albeck, op. cit., p. 12.

that of any Karaite group belongs to the same class of indirect evidence. It is certain nowadays that Karaism preserved much of older strata not only of non-Rabbinic, but also of Rabbinic Judaism.[1] The significance of any such survival depends, however, upon our ability to trace its origin to such an older group; the mere statement of its presence in Karaism has no heuristic value whatever. Moreover, as recent research has discovered a distinct possibility of the Qumran sect being itself one of the sources of Karaite thought,[2] cases where a feature can be found only in Qumran and in Karaism must not be taken, unless there is weighty evidence to the contrary, to indicate that the feature in question is older than the Qumran sect. The search for such agreement is part of the historiography of Karaism, not of Scrolls research.

Except for the little we can get out of Samaritans and Falashas, then, the study of the Qumran halakhah would thus be a barren field—for comparison is meaningless where there are only two things to compare, in this case Qumran and Rabbinic law—but for the fact that Rabbinic halakhah occasionally allows us glimpses into its own development, enabling us, by extrapolation, to relate Qumran practice to it.

It would be a vain undertaking to write a history of Jewish practice on the basis of the names of scholars to which, in controversies, various opinions are attached, since the opinions are often demonstrably older than the scholars in question, and the attributions merely show in which schools these traditions were preserved. Geiger's attempt to demonstrate that the school of Ishmael represented a more conservative system of law as compared with the school of Akiba must be considered as having failed—though of course it is generally admitted that the school of Ishmael represented a more conservative practice of legal argument.

Geiger, and even more so S. Frankel, inaugurated the more promising line of discovering the conditions under which halakhic practices could have arisen, or, as we might say, their *Sitz im Leben*. The latest, and most successful, application of this method is two articles by F. Baer[3] in which he demonstrated that certain

---

[1] Cf. Bar-Sasson, *Zion*, xv (1949–50), 42–55.
[2] Cf. Kahle, *VT* iii (1953), 82–84.
[3] *Luaḥ Haareẓ* for 1951–2; *Zion*, xvi (1951–2), 1–55.

parts of Rabbinic halakhah can best be understood in the context of the Maccabean period and as the result of the striving for an 'ideal state' in the Greek sense, a feature of Pharisaism already noticed by Josephus when he compares it to Stoicism.[1]

While none of the legal items dated by Baer happens to occur in Qumran literature so far published, his studies are of the greatest importance in showing that early Pharisaism envisaged—and idealized—the small agricultural community, much as do CDC and the traditions about the Holy Congregation. The social climate of the early Pharisaic group, as described by Baer, closely resembles the community of CDC.

It is of course true that this particular approach will often be dependent upon our theories about the social development and structure of the people at the time, and has something subjective about it. It would thus be dangerous to apply it in making comparisons with Qumran halakhah. Fortunately, Rabbinic halakhah itself sometimes indicates in various ways that an item is either old or of recent origin, and comparison with extra-Rabbinic sources, including the Qumran writings, enables us to see these matters in the proper light.

Quite frequently there is a definite statement to the effect that a certain practice was formerly different ('at first they used to . . . then they . . .')[2] or was deliberately introduced (*Takkanoth, Gĕzeroth*). This is not always reliable, since the Rabbis liked to date such rulings back to Ezra, &c., and probably we are often simply not informed that something is a new rule; for instance, in M. AZ 2. 4 the prohibition of gentile-made cheese is an established fact and the subject of a controversy about mid-second century, while the story of an incident before A.D. 130 (ibid. 2. 5) incidentally reveals it to have been a recent *Gĕzerah*. Actually, this class of items has little bearing on our problem, as few if any of them are represented in Qumran literature. One might perhaps mention the injunction to wash or perfume clothes for the Sabbath (CDC xi. 4), which is said to have been instituted by Ezra (B.T. BQ 82a).[3]

---

[1] *Vita* 2, at end.

[2] Often the difference is not in practice, but in formulation.

[3] It is, however, observed by the Falashas, cf. Leslau, op. cit., p. xxxiii.

Difficult problems are raised by the distinction between 'Biblical' (*min ha-Torah, middě'oraitha*) and 'Rabbinical' (*divrē sofĕrim, middĕrabbanan*) items of Rabbinic halakhah. In all probability the distinction is one of legal argument rather than of substance. Frequently the classification is a matter for discussion. Sometimes it seems as if it simply describes those rules for which even the school of Akiba had not found a satisfactory Biblical 'proof'. On the other hand, it has far-reaching practical consequences; e.g. 'Rabbinical' Sabbath transgressions are not punishable; a Rebellious Elder is executed for opposing 'Rabbinical' but not 'Biblical' rulings (M. San. 11. 3). In M. Hul. 8. 4 we find Akiba himself arguing that boiling of the meat of game and fowl with milk (which of course he considered inadmissible) is not a 'Biblical' prohibition.

The fact that we find in CDC quite a number of 'Rabbinical' items might thus be considered a proof of the closeness of its legislation to the Pharisaic-Rabbinic. There is no need here to repeat the details, which will be found in Ginzberg's *Unbekannte jüdische Sekte*; it should be added that the mention of the 'drink of the Many' in the novitiate rules in DSD constitutes another parallel, since the idea that drinkable fluids can receive uncleanness is 'Rabbinical', in contrast to the uncleanness of 'wet' produce, which is 'Biblical'. The value of this circumstance as evidence is, however, considerably reduced by the fact that 'Rabbinical' prohibitions play an important role among the Sabbath laws of both Jubilees and *Tě'ĕzāza Sanbat*, carrying the death penalty in the same way as do 'Biblical' prohibitions. It is, in my opinion, impossible to evaluate this aspect of the problem without an investigation of the whole complex of 'Biblical' and 'Rabbinical' legislation in Rabbinic Law.

There are, however, cases in which a legal innovation is not clearly stated, but discernible from the way in which the matter is presented. A fairly obvious case is B.T. Ber. 22a: 'A person who has had a seminal effusion is cleansed as soon as nine *kabs* of water have been poured over him. Nahum of Gimzo whispered this to R. Akiba, R. Akiba whispered it to Ben Azzai, and Ben Azzai went out and taught it to his disciples in the street.' The early Karaite writers 'Anan and Sahl b. Maẓliaḥ insist on the full waiting period till the evening and the ritual bath. That this is an old practice is proved by the statement of the Jew Trypho (Justin's *Dialogue*, i. 46) that after sexual intercourse it is necessary to bathe just as after 'touching things forbidden by Moses'. Here CDC xii. 22 takes up an intermediate position: it admits the 'washing' (*kbs*) instead of full immersion, but apparently prolongs the waiting period till the evening. M. Ber. 3. 5 permits prayers immediately after the immersion.

Again, the story about the 'rediscovery' by Hillel of the rule that the Passover Sacrifice is brought also on a Sabbath (Tos. Pes. 4. 1) may possibly hide an admission that the rule was changed only fairly late in the history of Pharisaism, and that in its older period the sect—like all other Jewish groups—did not admit the sacrifice on the Sabbath. The knowledge of this may lie behind R. Akiba's half-playful argument to the contrary (M. Pes. 6. 2) and account for R. Eliezer's unusually sharp and shocked reaction. CDC xi. 17–18 states the older rule in a very general way—not mentioning Passover at all—and brings Biblical evidence; this suggests that the subject was discussed at the time of the origin of CDC legislation.

Playful arguments of the kind just mentioned seem occasionally to reflect real controversies. CDC (x. 21; xi. 6) shows that the sect had a double Sabbath limit for different purposes: 1,000 and 2,000 cubits. This is in itself much more lenient than the practice of the Samaritans, *Tě'ēzāza Sanbat*, and Jubilees, as well as of the Karaites, all of whom forbid leaving the locality.[1] Rabbinic halakhah fixes the Sabbath limit at 2,000 cubits, but allows an extension to 4,000 cubits by the simple process of placing an object at the 2,000 cubit limit as an '*eruv*; indeed, a fourth-century teacher, R. Mana (P.T. Eru. iii, 21a bottom), refers to the 4,000 as if it were a normal limit, while another points out that the only limit with clear (*měhuwwar*) Biblical authority would be 12,000 cubits. The 2,000 cubit limit is attached to Num. xxxv. 5 by R. Akiba, but this derivation was rejected by R. Eliezer b. Yose the Galilean, who

---

[1] References in Albeck, op. cit., pp. 10, 43. Dr. J. Tubiana of Paris kindly informs me that the Falashas now walk as far as the nearest watercourse, but do not cross it.

thus took the limit to be purely 'Rabbinical'. In B.T. Eru. 51a, an Amora of the third century suggests, however, that the limit might just as well have been fixed after Num. xxxv. 4 at 1,000 cubits, and advances rather pedantic reasons for rejecting this. We may thus conclude that Rabbinic halakhah did its best to enlarge the Sabbath limit and—by declaring it to be 'Rabbinical'[1]—to soften its impact, but still recalled an earlier, stricter period.

Another symptom of change in law seems to be the insistence with which certain matters are put forward, and which no doubt served the same purpose as the habit of not divulging the reasons for new decrees (*gĕzeroth*) for twelve months, namely to prevent harmful public discussion.[2] Thus a Baraitha in B.T. Yeb. 62b–63a declares a man who has married his sister's daughter to be a special favourite of the Lord, and applies to him, along with those who love their neighbours and relatives and lend money to the poor, the first half of Isa. lviii. 9. Similarly, Tos. Qid. 1. 4 prescribes: 'a man should not marry until his sister's daughter grows up or he finds a wife suitable to his station'.[3] Why should such an unequal marriage be so strongly recommended, unless it was to counteract popular feeling which was against it, in keeping with the unanimous condemnation of such marriages by Samaritans, Falashas, the Church, the Karaites, and Islam?[4]

The key is provided by Josephus. He tells of one case of niece-marriage in the priestly family of the Tobiads (*Ant.* XII. iv. 6) and no less than six in the family of Herod: his uncle Joseph with Herod's sister Salome (*BJ* I. xxii. 4); Herod himself with a daughter of his brother and a daughter of his sister (*Ant.* XVII. i. 3); his son Philip with Salome, daughter of Herodias (*Ant.* XVIII. v. 4); Herodias with two of her uncles successively (*Ant.* XVIII. v. 1); her other daughter Berenice with her uncle Herod of Chalkis (*Ant.* XIX.

---

[1] Albeck, loc. cit.   [2] Cf. Danby's note on M. AZ 2. 5.

[3] ‏לא ישא אדם עד שתגדיל בת אחותו או עד שימצא את ההוגנת לו‎. This is to my knowledge the only text in Jewish literature enjoining a delay of marriage. As it is actually followed by proofs for the undesirability of remaining unmarried for too long, I wonder whether some words have not fallen out, and we should read: ‏לא [ימתין] אדם [עד ש]ישא אשה עד שתגדיל בת אחותו או עד שימצא...‎. It would still permit niece-marriage, or even mark it as a widespread practice.

[4] References in Krauss, 'Die Ehe zwischen Onkel und Nichte', *Kohler Festschrift* (1913), pp. 167–8.

v. 1). Amongst the hundreds of Tannaitic teachers, on the other hand, only one case is known, that of Eliezer b. Hyrcanus who married his sister's daughter against his will, having been practically compelled to do so by the girl (Aboth R. Nathan, ch. 16, f. 32a) or by his own mother and the girl together (P.T. Yeb. xiii. 2, 13c). There is at least one tradition which makes R. Eliezer a priest (P.T. Sot. iii. 4, 19a).[1] In any event, the story is curious, because a well-authenticated tradition makes his wife Imma-Shalom, the sister of R. Gamaliel the Patriarch (B.T. BM 56b), and since according to P.T. Eliezer's mother was still alive, he can hardly have been very old at the time, as Hyman suggests (op. cit., p. 169).

The practice, in any case, appears to have been current among the aristocracy and the priests, both groups where the choice of a suitable partner was limited, and was thus in all probability countenanced by Sadducee halakhah. With the Pharisees it was either completely forbidden, or there were strong scruples.[2] The Rabbis, however, when faced with the alternative of disqualifying numbers of priests or legalizing past niece-marriages, took refuge behind a literal interpretation of the Biblical incest laws and allayed the uneasiness of their own followers by making it a particularly meritorious type of union. I would suggest that the choice of Isa. lviii. 9, rather than any other verse promising reward, is in fact occasioned by the second half of that verse: 'If thou take away from the midst of thee injustice,[3] the putting forth of the finger and speaking vanity', i.e. people who see such a marriage are enjoined not to engage in malicious gossip. It is possibly for this reason that Othniel b. Kenaz, the judge, was not only by an ingenious combination made the husband of his niece, but was at the same time—for no visible reason—extolled as a particularly pious and learned man and an ascetic (B.T. Tem.

---

[1] For evidence against it, see Hyman, Tolĕdhoth Tanna'im wa-Amora'im, pp. 162–3.

[2] As Krauss (op. cit.) points out, such scruples are reflected in M. Ned. 8. 7; 9. 10. I am at a loss to understand Kohler's statement (JQR v (1892–3), 406, n. 1): 'Throughout the Book of Jubilees . . . the rule is maintained that each pious man should marry the daughter of his brother or sister.' Kohler gives no references; some are provided by Krauss, op. cit., p. 175, but the only one of these which I have been able to trace speaks of marriage between cousins.

[3] See Ben-Yehudah, Thesaurus, vi. 2841; but probably to be read muṭṭeh.

16a, &c.), perhaps because the ascetics and pietists were the chief opponents of such marriages. However, only the Gaonic Halakhoth Gedoloth (ed. Hildesheimer, p. 609) use this historical 'fact'—in complete contradiction to Rabbinic rules—as proof for the *permissibility* of the practice, which they say was then rejected by the Minim (probably the Karaites); it is possible, however, to see here the reflection of an old controversy against real Minim, the Qumran sect.

Now CDC v. 7–11 not merely states that niece-marriage is forbidden, and proves it from the Pentateuch, but it accuses the 'builders of the wall' of actually doing so. The accusation is thus levelled either at the Sadducees, or at those who countenanced Sadducee practices by making them appear as 'kinds of righteousness' (iv. 16–17), and who are 'caught in the net' (ibid. 18–19), a phrase which DST iv. 12 clearly shows to mean being misled by false interpretations.

The two other practices appearing in CDC v in conjunction with niece-marriage are polygamy—which as far as we know was non-existent among the Rabbis, but must have been more common among the wealthy classes and priests, as shown also by Josephus—and 'conveying uncleanness to the sanctuary', which of course is specifically aimed at priests, and is in keeping with the accusations levelled against them in other Pharisaic writings, such as the Psalms of Solomon and the Testaments of the Patriarchs.

If we add to this the relaxation of the rules excluding publicans, criminals, and gamblers,[1] we can see that for the more conservative-minded among the Pharisees there were enough reasons for dissatisfaction. Geiger[2] thought that the Pharisees in the course of their history moved away from Sadducee practice. This may be true in some respects, but there is also evidence—at a certain stage at least—of a tendency towards a *rapprochement* with Sadduceeism.

In Rabbinic controversy with Sadducee views, the underlying assumption is that the Sadducees go wrong through ignorance, not that they pervert teaching which they have received. In the arguments of CDC and DST against the sect's opponents, the assumption is that the false teachers know full well what the Law is, but

---

[1] Ch. IV, p. 64.　　　　　　[2] *Jüdische Zeitschrift*, ii (1863), 12.

pervert it. This accusation is most easily understood if we assume that the practices the sect condemned were recent innovations, 'removals of the boundary': the opponents had themselves acted according to the right law and deviated from it. We are not concerned here with the justice of this accusation, but it would not have been possible to make it unless there had been *some* changes. Moreover, it is the accusation of someone within the same movement, not of an outsider, who would have objected to the whole body of Pharisee tenets, not to certain minor features.

VII

THE MAKING OF LAW

WHERE the substance of the Law was concerned, we were considerably hampered by the paucity of information on non-Rabbinic systems, which in most cases makes it impossible to decide whether a similarity between Qumran and Rabbinic halakhah is of any significance. The situation is quite different when we come to the formal aspects of halakhah. Here it is quite certain that the methods of discussion and the terminology were to a large extent developed in the Pharisaic and Rabbinic schools. Josephus (*Ant.* XVIII. i. 4), indeed, remarks that the Sadducees 'reckon it a virtue to argue with the teachers of wisdom', διδασκάλους σοφίας,[1] but this should not be taken as evidence that there was much common ground, for the commentary on *Megillath Ta'anith*[2] is surely right in saying that 'they could not bring proofs from the Pentateuch' but were content to consult their 'Book of Decrees'. The great achievement of Pharisaism was precisely that in its methods of interpretation (*midrash*) it had discovered a means of making the Law reasonable and of adapting it to the needs of the time.[3] Any similarity in these formal matters must therefore weigh heavily in placing the sect of Qumran within Judaism. It is proposed in this chapter to treat this under two headings: the general technique of arriving at a legal decision and the validity of the law thus made, and the terminology and presentation of the material.

Josephus already points out two essential features of the Pharisee attitude to the Law: that they strove to observe it in all details (*BJ* II. i. 14; *Ant.* XVII. ii. 4; *Vita* 38), and that they observed laws (νόμιμα) not written in the Law of Moses, but handed down from ancient times (*Ant.* XIII. x. 6): the example given refers to a case of greater

---

[1] = 'pupils of the wise' in Rabbinic parlance?

[2] Neubauer, *Mediaeval Jewish Chronicles*, i. 8.

[3] J. Z. Lauterbach, *Kohler Festschrift* (1913), pp. 186 seq., has shown that the Sadducees did not reject tradition as such, but unlike the Pharisees did not attempt to attach it to the written Law.

leniency in capital punishment. Although the name of the Essenes is mentioned in the last-named passage, Josephus does not say that they too followed such ancient traditional laws; he does, however, say (*BJ* ii. viii. 5) that their prayers were inherited (πάτριοι).

With regard to the ἀκρίβεια in observing the laws, the Qumran sect stands on the same level as the Pharisees and the Rabbinic community. The rules in CDC fix everything in minute detail, including the indication of measurements. The sect also shares with the Pharisees the attachment to the additional laws handed down from the ancients. This is not only visible in the practical sphere, many of the rules being evidently part of the traditional supplementation of Biblical legislation, but is expressly stated in CDC i. 16 where the opponents are accused of 'removing the landmark which the ancients (*rishonim*) have set up in their inheritance'. The comparison of 'Rabbinical' law with the boundary between fields, the 'fence', is, of course, common in Rabbinic writings. Eccl. x. 8, 'whoso breaketh through a fence, a serpent shall bite him', was so currently explained as describing the punishment for 'Rabbinical' transgressions that it gave rise to the phrase 'the serpent of the Rabbis has bitten him' (B.T. Shab. 11a, &c.).

There is no need here to go into the complicated question of the attachment of Rabbinic law to the Pentateuch with its many gradations, from the outright 'Rabbinical', via the 'Halakhah given to Moses on Sinai' and the traditional, but far from obvious, 'interpretations', the cases where 'although there is no proof of the matter there is an indication', to the more or less involved scriptural proofs. The legislation in CDC offers cases of almost all of these: it sometimes offers scriptural proof in the form of quotations, at other times the proof is implied in the phraseology, borrowed from the relevant scriptural passage with slight but significant changes; in many cases no scriptural proof is attempted. The phrases with which the quotations are introduced are—as with Rabbinic writings—the same for 'aggadah' and halakhah, and can all be matched from Rabbinic usage, though the ones normally used in Qumran are not those normally used in Rabbinic literature, and vice versa. Thus *ka'ăsher amar*, the most common formula, does not occur in Rabbinic style, which uses either

the present tense, or much more frequently the passive *shenne'ĕmar*
(*ἐρρέθη* in Matt.). The phrase *ka'ăsher kathuv* (CDC vii. 19; DSD
v. 17) does not correspond exactly to the common Rabbinic *kakka-
thuv*, but rather to *kĕdhikhĕthiv*, the Aramaic formula which so often
appears in Hebrew contexts. Once we have *ki khen kathuv* (DSD
v. 15), corresponding to the very rare *shehărē kathuv* (cf. Bacher,
Die exegetische Terminologie, p. 88, n. 5) and occurring in the same
form as in DSD in the late Deut. Rabba, *Niẓẓavim* i. The author-
ship of a prophet is indicated CDC iv. 13 by the phrase 'as He spoke
through (*bĕyadh*) Isaiah' (possibly the same was written CDC
xix. 7), for which Bacher, op. cit., p. 68, has only one example,
but which corresponds to 'that which is spoken through the prophet . . . saying', so frequent in Matthew.

The scriptural proofs are, however, never elaborately stated—
no doubt because in the works at our disposal the purpose is strictly
practical—except where it is a matter of controversy. What a full-
fledged scriptural argument looked like, we can see from the
example in CDC v. 8–11.

It should be noted that one of the methods of exegesis is that of
'inclusion and exclusion', which Rabbinic literature is unanimous
in connecting specifically with R. Akiba, who learned it from
Nahum of Gimzo (cf. Gen. Rabba 1. 14). It is expressly stated in
xi. 18, but implied in ix. 5 and other places. This is hardly a
coincidence, for in its whole approach to the question of Biblical
attachment CDC goes with R. Akiba rather than with R. Ishmael. In
view of the connexions between R. Akiba and a group somewhat
similar to the Qumran sect, which we have observed in Chapter III,
we may ask ourselves whether this particular system of exegesis did
not originate with Messianic sects of this type. In order to provide
the scriptural proof for their theories of history, an interpretation
of 'every crown of each letter' (B.T. Men. 29b) naturally resulted
from it, and produced the state of mind and the skill necessary for
the refined methods of halakhic exegesis associated with R. Akiba.

One of the important results of R. Akiba's innovations was that
the traditional-authoritative element in halakhah was weakened.[1]

---

[1] Cf. W. Bacher, *Kohler Festschrift*, p. 59, who demonstrates that in the Akiba
school the term 'Halakhah given to Moses on Sinai' had lost all meaning, being
employed vaguely as a term for all oral law.

Though no change in actual substance took place, the Rabbinic school was henceforth not a place where series of regulations were learnt by rote from the mouth of teachers, but a place for discussion in which all could take part because the basis was equally available to all. This is exactly the feature most prominent in the law-making of the Qumran sect, as described in its writings.[1]

Some passages, it is true, might create the impression that law was entirely in the hands of the priests. These are CDC xiii. 2–4 and DSD ix. 7. The former runs: 'And in a place of ten, let there not be absent a man, a priest,[2] instructed in the Book of the *Hagi*, on his mouth they shall all kiss.' The last phrase is from Gen. xli. 40, and rendered by LXX, Pesh., Vulg.: 'according to his word they shall all be ruled'. The Targums explain 'according to his command they shall eat', and this is in my view the more probable meaning here.[3] The number ten is needed only for communal ceremonies, especially for the common meals, where an authoritative knowledge of the laws of purity is needed. This is why, if the priest is ignorant, a Levite can take his place.

The second passage states: 'Only the sons of Aaron shall have power over judgement and property, and according to them shall the lot go forth for all the number of the men of the Community.' Here the context shows clearly that a future state of affairs ('And when these things will be in Israel') is meant, namely the time when the community will 'separate themselves amongst the council of the men of injustice so as to go into the desert' (DSD viii. 13), the time immediately before the final battle against the Kittim, which will take place 'when the exiles of the sons of light shall return from the desert of the nations' (DSW i. 3). It is not quite clear why just at that period the priests will have additional powers:

---

[1] A protest against teaching by authority may be contained in DST vi. 13–14, as restored by M. Wallenstein, *J. Rylands Bull.* xxxviii (1955), 247: 'There is no mediating teacher for Thy congregation, and no one to pronounce teaching (*meshiv*) as an announcement (*kĕruz*); for they are the congregation of Thy counsel, and they will pronounce teaching according to (*bĕ-fi* = *'al-pi*) Thy glory.' For *meliẓ* = teacher, see above, p. 55; for *kĕruz*, cf. DST v. 36, 'heralds (*kĕrazĕ*) of sin, changing the works of God through their guilt'. For *meshiv*, cf. DSD v. 2.

[2] The normal way of addressing a priest was apparently *ishi kohen*, M. Yoma i. 3; B.T. Nid. 33b.

[3] I.e. they must not eat before he has pronounced the blessing, cf. p. 35.

possibly because it is a period of intensified purification, or because a return to the Biblical idea of the priest as teacher was
thought theoretically desirable.

For the time being, during the 'epoch of wickedness' and until
the coming of the 'epoch of Thy glory' (DST xii. 22), the Law is
not fully known to mankind; many things are 'hidden' to all
Israel, so that it goes astray (CDC iii. 14; DSD v. 11)—though
DSD v. 12 points out that the sect's opponents were none too
careful about observing the 'uncovered' laws either. The sect
has succeeded in 'uncovering' a number of these hidden laws
(CDC iii. 14) concerning the correct observance of Sabbaths
and Festivals, &c. 'The uncovered ones' becomes practically
synonymous with 'laws', e.g. DSD i. 9 (cf. CDC ii. 16) or CDC
xv. 13.

The way in which these discoveries are made is, of course,
midrash, the sect's peculiar method of scripture interpretation.
The following passage seems to refer not to halakhah, but according to the context to the finding of Messianic indications, but as
pointed out before, the two exegetical processes are the same:
'And any thing which was hidden from Israel, and has been found
by the man who interprets, let him not hide it from these because
of a cowardly spirit' (DSD viii. 12). The verb 'to be found' occurs
frequently in connexion with the observation of the laws: 'to
return to the Law of Moses . . . to that which is found to be done
in the whole epoch of wickedness' (CDC xv. 9–10); 'to teach them
all that is found to be done in this time' (DSD ix. 20), &c.

In the course of a discussion about death, B.T. Shab. 151b
quotes a saying by the contemporary of R. Judah the Prince,
Simeon b. Eleazar:[1] 'Do as long as you find and it is found
(= available) to you, and you are still in your own hand.' This
forms the beginning of a digression on the difference between the
present age and the time after the coming of the Messiah, the first
statement of which is: 'in the days of the Messiah there will be
neither merit nor guilt'. The structure of the passage suggests that
this forms the end of the saying of Simeon b. Eleazar, and that it

[1] Perhaps, as Yose b. Meshullam appears in controversy with him, he was
close to the Holy Congregation.

—and the ensuing discussion—was inserted under the mistaken impression that it referred to individual death. It obviously has a bearing on the meaning of 'to find' in the Qumran writings.

One might at first be tempted to translate the verb as 'to be able', except that this hardly fits the character of a sect which was prepared to go to the greatest lengths to observe all laws. It might be objected that after the destruction of the Temple, sacrifices, &c., had to be in abeyance, but the sect—as to some extent Rabbinic Judaism—had efficiently compensated for this by prayer and the observation of supererogatory purity laws. It can, however, be shown that 'to find' refers to the knowledge of the laws. In the prescriptions for the teacher in DSD ix. 12, he is enjoined: 'to do the will of God according to all that is uncovered from time to time, and to teach[1] all the intelligence[2] which is found according to the times'. The members are obliged to keep 'the appointed times and the fast day according to the finding of them that entered the New Covenant in the land of Damascus' (CDC vi. 18–19). 'To find' thus means to evolve new law, or rather to 'uncover' the true meaning of the Law as written or handed down. It is in a way a synonym of 'to uncover', as is seen by confronting DSD v. 9 with CDC xv. 10.

This implies that the Law is not fixed for all time—as the Sadducees thought—but constantly evolves. This, of course, is a through and through Rabbinic idea, most beautifully expressed in the story in B.T. Men. 29b, where Moses comes to a lecture of R. Akiba and 'did not know what he (Akiba) was talking', but is in the end assured that it is all 'halakhah given to Moses on Sinai'. A further implication is that in our own time the Law is not yet fully known. Rabbinic discussion, by deferring the solution of problems where no decision can be reached 'until Elijah shall come and solve it', represents the same point of view.

In each of the colophons which conclude a series of laws in CDC, there is a reference to the Messianic advent: 'And this is the disposition of the session of the camps, that walk in these during the epoch of wickedness until there arise the Messiah of Aaron and

---

[1] Read *ulĕlammed*.
[2] On *śekhel* = religious knowledge, cf. p. 4.

Israel' (xii. 23–xiii. 1);[1] 'And this is the session of the camps for all [the epoch of wickedness]' (followed by the Messianic verse Isa. vii. 17) (xiii. 20–xiv. 1); 'And this is the account of the session of the [   ] and this is the account of the rulings in which [they shall walk during the epoch of wickedness until there arise the Messia]h of Aaron and Israel and make conciliation for their trespasses' (xiv. 17–19).

The rulings are thus only for the time until the coming of the Messiah; then a new disposition will come into force. From the general tenor of the statements in the Qumran writings, it appears that this will be a complete knowledge of the Law, without any uncertainties. This, I would suggest, is the explanation of the mysterious statement that the Messiah will make conciliation for their trespasses. The same expression occurs in CDC iii. 18–19: 'But God in His wonderful mysteries made conciliation for their trespass and pardoned their impiety.' The context there shows clearly that the 'trespass' was committed out of ignorance of the true Law, and the 'conciliation' was part of the establishment of correct Law. The phrase therefore need mean no more than that after the revelation of the Divine halakhah the members of the sect will be forgiven any errors committed because of the imperfection of their human halakhah. It may, of course, mean more.

The above statement by Simeon b. Eleazar is by no means the only one announcing the cessation of halakhah as we understand it (merit and guilt) after the coming of the Messiah. Ben Zoma is quoted as saying (P.T. Ber. i. 9, 4a): 'Israel will in the future (i.e. after the Messiah) not mention the Exodus from Egypt any longer.'[2] As the mention of the Exodus is a Pentateuchal law, this envisages the abolition at least of some laws. The mystical *Alphabethā dĕ-R. Akiba* (Jellinek's *Beth ha-Midrash*, iii. 27) states that the Messiah will reveal a new Torah. As will be seen, the conception is not widespread in Rabbinic literature, which generally looks upon the activity of Elijah mentioned above as a mere filling-up of some very minor gaps; in fact, the entire framework

[1] This seems preferable to the rendering in *ZD*, where I had taken 'until . . .' as the beginning of the next paragraph.

[2] In the discussion, Jer. xvi. 15 is quoted. This verse mentions the return from the 'land of the north'—the sect's term for its temporary abode (CDC vii. 14).

must be imagined as persisting if the solution of these difficulties is to have any sense. The idea of the New Law is thus likely to have been restricted to certain mystical circles, and the appearance of Ben Zoma among its adherents is significant.

Meanwhile, the Law keeps its secrets and yields them up only to some extent. The term 'secrets of the Law' is quite common in Rabbinic parlance,[1] and we hear in particular of *mĕgilloth sĕtharim*, 'scrolls of secrets', from which we get some quotations on minor points of law. We have an interesting example of such a quotation in B.T. BM 92a: 'Rab said, I found a scroll of secrets in the house of R. Ḥiyya, and in it was written: Issi b. Judah says, "When thou comest into thy neighbour's vineyard, then thou mayest eat grapes thy fill at thine own pleasure . . ." (Deut. xxiii. 24)—the verse applies to everyone', i.e. not only to workers employed in the vineyard, as was the Rabbinic interpretation.[2] P.T. Maas. ii. 6, 50a, the same view is given in the name of Issi b. 'Akabiah without any mention of secret scrolls; there was thus nothing secret about the doctrine or the scroll.[3] On the other hand, the somewhat revolutionary character of the doctrine—Rab rightly adds: 'Issi has left no one any livelihood'—suggests its origin in a circle with social doctrines not held by the majority, possibly a group with agricultural ideals such as the Holy Congregation. This does not mean that all 'scrolls of secrets' emanated from such circles.

The legal section of CDC is divided into a number of sections, each with a separate colophon mentioning its connexion with a 'session' (*moshab*). These sections may well give us an idea what a 'scroll of secrets' was like, for none is a complete presentation of a legal subject, but they consist in individual rules intended to fill in gaps within an existing system of practice. It may not be amiss to remind ourselves that the only reason that we understand most, at any rate, of these rules is the fact that the general system into which they fit is so similar to the Rabbinic one, otherwise the Sabbath laws in particular would have been a closed book to us.

---

[1] References in *ZD*, p. 12.
[2] Cf. J. H. Heinemann, *HUCA* xxv (1954), 311.
[3] This disposes of the theory that the secret scrolls were kept hidden because it was forbidden to commit halakhah to writing.

What, then, was the occasion for collecting these rules in such
a form, and from what body did they issue?

The *moshab*, 'session', occurs five times in CDC, four times in
connexion with such series of laws. Apart from xiv. 17, where the
next word is destroyed, it is the 'session of (all xiv. 3) the camps';
in xii. 19 the 'session of the cities of Israel'. In DSD it is either just
'session' or 'the session of the Many'. Comparison of DSD vi. 8
with CDC xiv. 3 proves that all these terms mean one and the same
thing. Several rules in DSD vii regulate the behaviour of members
during the session; line 11 shows clearly that the session lasted
a limited time and was a recurrent event. The description in DSD
vi. 8–13 also shows that certain matters of policy were discussed
during these sessions; it moreover establishes that 'the Many' can
serve as a synonym for 'the session of the Many'.

Here the laws we find in CDC were discussed, and no doubt
formally issued as scrolls at the end of the session. The session had,
however, other functions: it administered the group's finances
(CDC xiv. 12 seqq.), it accepted new members (DSD vi. 13 seqq.),
and it acted as a court of law (DSD vii. 21, &c.).

Rabbinic Judaism had an institution which similarly combined the
functions of a place of halakhic discussion and a court of law. This
was the *yeshibah*. There is no need here to add to the descriptions of
these institutions given in works on the Tannaitic period. Attention
should perhaps be drawn to the fact that the scholion in *Megillath
Ta'anith* (ed. Neubauer, p. 17) uses the verb 'to sit' as denoting membership of the great Synhedrion in Jerusalem in Hasmonean times.

'Yeshibah' in Tannaitic parlance is synonymous with *beth
midrash* and with *beth din*: the first stresses the 'interpretative'
aspect, the second the judiciary function. However, even *beth din*
is occasionally used of the teaching institution, e.g. the *beth din* or
beth midrash of Shem and Eber (Gen. Rabba 63. 10)[1] and of
Methuselah, also called the *midrash* of Methuselah.[2] In Qumran
parlance, this is reflected by the double sense of *darash* and *midrash*. On the one hand, they refer to the study and interpretation
of the Law, on the other, *darash* means 'to examine' a person as to

[1] See Ginzberg, *Legends*, v. 192.
[2] Maimonides, *Guide*, ii. 39; source unknown, cf. Ginzberg, *Legends*, v. 166.

his suitability for the sect (DSD vi. 14, 17), synonymous with
paqadh (CDC xiii. 11), and *midrash ha-torah*, which in DSD viii.
15 means 'interpretation', means in CDC xx. 6 'judicial investigation'; cf. also DSD vi. 24.

Both in the *moshab* and in the *yeshibah* the seating was in a fixed
order (DSD vi. 8; CDC xiv. 6; M. San. 4. 3–4), and as the members
of the *moshab* were asked their opinion each in turn (loc. cit. and
DSD vi. 10), so the members of the *beth din* when functioning as
a court of law were asked in order of seating (M. San. 4. 2), so also
in one case of purity (Tos. Ohol. 4. 2).

In the *beth din* as a court decisions were taken by vote; this was
called 'to stand up for counting' (M. San. 5. 5, &c.). Voting, however, was also used not infrequently when there were differences
on ritual or other halakhic matters; often such votes were taken
on a whole series of unconnected matters, much in the way the
moshab of the Qumran sect did in the lists in CDC; such lists are
usually quoted with indication of the place where and occasion on
which the voting took place. One of the earliest is the eighteen
decisions 'which the Sages enjoined while they were in the upper
room of Hananiah b. Hezekiah b. Gorion, when they went up to
visit (?) him' (M. Shab. 1. 4); perhaps the latest was the great
meeting at Usha, after the end of the Hadrianic war, when many
outstanding problems were settled. For that meeting we have some
information as to the way participants were summoned: 'they sent
to the elders of Galilee and said: whoever has studied, let him
come and teach, and whoever has not studied, let him come and
learn' (Cant. Rabba on ii. 5). We also have an account of the
solemn opening of the meeting, with sermons.[1] The whole atmo-
sphere of Usha is one not unlike the *moshab ha-rabbim* of the
Qumran sect. Such conferences do not suddenly arise out of
nothing. For their success they require a certain tradition of
organization and procedure, and the evidently smooth functioning
of the Usha conference strongly suggests that it continued a
custom current before 130. We hear a great deal about the decisions
taken in 'the vineyard at Jamnia' (B.T. Ber. 63b). A meeting in the
open air suggests large crowds: it may thus have been a meeting

---

[1] Cf. Weiss, *Dor dor wě-dorěshaw*, ii. 145.

similar to that at Usha; so perhaps was the meeting in the upper
room of Hananiah, long before the destruction of the Temple.
All this points to an established Pharisee custom of meetings where
legal matters were decided by vote.

The decisive passage for the practice of the Qumran sect in these
matters is DSD v. 2 seq.: 'who pronounce teaching[1] according to
the sons of Zadok, the priests, the keepers of the covenant,[2] and[3]
according to the majority of the men of the Community who hold
fast to the covenant; according to them shall the order of the lot go
forth for everything: for the Law, for property, and for judgement . . .'. The word 'majority', *rov*, is rendered as 'assembly' by
Delcor (*RB* lxi (1954), 534) and Lambert (*Anal. Lovan.* ii. 963),
but it never has that meaning: it means 'multitude' in Biblical
and 'majority' in Mishnaic Hebrew. The superscript 'and' before
'majority' appears to be wrong; if there had really been an 'and',
we should expect the second 'according to' to have been omitted.
If the 'and' is deleted, we find that the 'priests' are themselves
subordinate to the 'majority of the men of the Community'. The
priests are thus only an executive body.[4]

If there was a majority, there must have been voting. An allusion
to this may possibly exist in DSD vii. 10–12: 'And likewise the
man who is absent from the session of the Many not according
to a resolution and without good cause three times during one
session shall be punished for ten days, and if they *stand up and
he is absent, he shall be punished for thirty days.' The asterisked
word is יזקפו, the *qoph* being written above an erasure. The
Qal of *zqp* is transitive, 'to make erect' in Biblical and Mishnaic
Hebrew and in Accadian; the intransitive meaning 'to stand'
occurs occasionally in Mishnaic texts (cf. Ben Yehudah, *Thesaurus*, iii. 1387b), but the form encountered here is most probably
the Mishnaic Niph'al (= Christian Palest. Aram. Ethpe'el) in the
sense of 'to stand up from a sitting, &c., position'.[5] It is thus

---

[1] Cf., for this term, p. 98, n. 1. The origin was no doubt from the practice of
asking each one his opinion.

[2] In CDC iv. 1 these are equated with the latter-day elect.

[3] Written above the line.   [4] Cf. also Ch. I, p. 8.

[5] Most of the explanations of this word hitherto advanced require an object
suffix or a dative after it.

synonymous with *'amadh*, i.e. the verb of the Mishnaic phrase for
'to vote'. An absence during vote-taking would of course be considerably more serious than absence during ordinary deliberations.

It may be pointed out here that the decision of a legal point by
voting was a somewhat archaic procedure in Rabbinic Judaism. After
Usha we do not hear much of such cases. One reason for its dis-
appearance was probably the more developed method of argument
in the school of R. Akiba, which made it possible to convince the opponent or find a compromise, but another, much more important
reason was the development of the scholastic approach which turned
difference of opinion into a virtue. On many matters the Mishnah
already cites two or more mutually exclusive views. In the Amoraic
period these school opinions formed the very basis of halakhic edu-
cation. The pattern is one familiar, for instance, in the development
of Muslim law or Arabic grammatical science, where after an initial
period of search for one truth there followed the study of differences
of opinion (*ikhtilāf*) as an intellectual discipline in its own right.

In Rabbinic parlance the result of a decision, whether arrived
at by vote or by argument, is called *hălākhāh*,[1] a verbal noun like
ămānāh, *dĕmāmāh*. It is not used in any other than the technical
sense, while the corresponding Aramaic term *hilkhĕthā* also means,
in the Targum, 'step', like the Christian Palest. Aramaic and
Syriac words of the same form. It has no derivation in Mishnaic
Hebrew: its semantic background is in fact provided by the
Qumran writings. There we find, on the one hand, *hălakhah*
used as an ordinary verbal noun of *halakh* (DSD i. 25; iii. 9), on
the other hand, *hithhallekh bĕ-* in the sense of 'act in accord with'
laws and statutes, 'follow' rules (e.g. DSD ix. 12 = CDC xii. 20;
CDC xx. 6, &c.), which is, of course, no more than a technical
development of the Biblical idiom 'to walk (Qal or Hithp.) in
the laws of the Lord'.

It will thus be seen that the *moshab ha-rabbim* and the Rabbinic
academy had much in common in procedure and nomenclature.
There is, however, at first sight one considerable difference: the
Rabbinic academy, by its very name, was a preserve of the learned

---

[1] In some cases 'halakhah' is an abbreviation for 'halakhah given to Moses on
Sinai', as opposed to later accretions. This, of course, is purely Rabbinic.

few, while the descriptions of the *moshab* seem to imply that all members of the sect took part. Actually, both the invitation to the Usha meeting (p. 104) and the numbers given of Akiba's pupils, 12,000 and 24,000 (B.T. Ket. 62b), suggest a much wider popular participation in these academies. We must, however, ask ourselves whether it is really certain that the *moshab* included all members of the sect. The system of asking everyone's opinion makes it very improbable that there were such large numbers present; the fines for absence suggest a small assembly in which every man counted; the way in which decisions are recorded implies that they had to be communicated to those who were not present when they were made.

I would suggest that a recollection of the real procedure is pre-served in a curious passage at the end of M. San. 1. 6: 'And how many should there be in a city that it may be fit to have a Sanhedrin (of twenty-three members)? A hundred and twenty men. R. Nehemiah (a contemporary of R. Meir) says: two hundred and thirty, corresponding to chiefs of ten.' Against the Rabbinic back-ground, these chiefs of ten are simply a picturesque and meaning-less evocation of a Biblical term (Exod. xviii. 21). Only in the Qumran sect were chiefs of ten the lowest class of officers (DSW iv. 5) who no doubt kept in constant touch with the ten men whose names were inscribed on their banners (ibid.). Moreover, only with the Qumran sect was the court of law at the same time the administrative authority, while the question of the relation be-tween the judiciary Sanhedrin of the Rabbis and the administrative Synhedrion of Josephus is a well-known crux of the history of post-Biblical Judaism. The idea that a court of law should be composed of administrative officials could not have arisen within Rabbinic Judaism at all. It must therefore represent an echo of an older order of things, i.e. presumably that of the Pharisaic assemblies or synhedria—note that συνέδριον translates *moshab* or *yeshibah*. We would thus learn, indirectly, that the older Pharisees, like the Qumran sect, had chiefs of ten, and thus also all the higher apparatus of chiefs of fifties, hundreds, thousands, and myriads.

Was the *moshab ha-rabbim* composed of chiefs of ten? I have not found anything in the texts to confirm or disprove it, but it is a possibility which must be kept in mind if we try to visualize the workings of the sect in practical terms.

It is difficult to estimate exactly to what extent the similarities in structure and procedure between the legislative bodies of the Qumran sect and Rabbinic Judaism force upon us the assumption of a common origin. It is quite different when we come to the terminology of legal argument. Here we cannot fail to be struck by the far-reaching similarity between the terminology of the legal chapters of CDC and Rabbinic literature. This similarity becomes all the more remarkable if we compare these two, for instance, with the halakhic disquisitions of Philo. Although the difference in substance between Philo and the Rabbis is small, his whole presentation and argumentation is utterly different.

The equality between Qumran and Rabbinic halakhah in terminology is not in the use of the same words. It lies in the fact that to the vast majority of the Qumran terms exact parallels can be found in Tannaitic legal language, though in almost every single instance the actual words used differ. To give only a few instances: the distinction between capital and property cases (Rabbinic *dinē nĕfashoth—dinē mamonoth*, Q. *dĕvar maweth—hon*, CDC ix. 17, 22), between intentional and unintentional violations of the law (R. *bĕ-mezidh—bi-shĕghaghah*, Q. *bĕ-yadh ramah—bi-rĕmiyyah*, but once *bi-shĕghaghah*, DSD viii. 24), between running water and drawn water (R. *mayim shĕ'uvim*, Q. *mēmē ha-kĕli*, CDC x. 13), between seminal effusion and other forms of uncleanness, requiring respectively washing (R. *rḥẓ*, Q. *kbs*) and bathing (R. *ṭbl*, Q. *rḥẓ*); the concept of *muqẓeh* (untouchable on the Sabbath)—though the term does not occur, the same verb as in Rabbinic terminology, *herim* (xi. 11), is used for it; *hoshi'ah yadho lo* (CDC ix. 10), R. (B.T.) *'āvidh dinā lĕ-nafsheh*. It is possible that Q. distinguished between 'Biblical' and 'Rabbinical' rules; a man who had transgressed anything of *Torath Mosheh* could never be readmitted (DSD viii. 22), while one who has violated the *miẓwah* is excluded only for a period of time (ibid. 17; cf. CDC xx. 3). Since the 'Torah of Moses' cannot be anything but 'Biblical' law, the 'commandment' must denote a less hallowed category. On the other hand, we do not find anywhere that the rulings made by the session of the Many are designated as *miẓwah*. In the only passages where the wording can be clearly established they are referred to as *ḥuqqim* (DSD ix. 12; CDC xii. 20) and *mishpaṭim* (CDC xii. 19). In Rabbinic literature there are several discussions as to the distinction between *ḥoq*, *miẓwah*, and *mishpaṭ*, involving the difference between written and oral law (e.g. B.T. Yoma 67b).

Under this class we must also include those cases in which certain Biblical terms are employed in a technical sense based upon some not at all self-evident interpretation. Thus *shamor* (Deut. v. 12) is used both in R. and in Q. (CDC x. 15–17) to demand an extension of Sabbath rest beyond the solar day; the interpretation of *zonah* in Lev. xxi. 7 as a woman who has broken the incest laws is taken up in CDC iv. 20 in the designation *zĕnuth* for incest (cf. the note in *ZD*, p. 17).

A particularly instructive example of this is the law about carrying on the Sabbath. It should first of all be noted that the absolute prohibition of carrying is Am-Haareẓ (Samaritans and Falashas) and Pharisee, but probably not Sadducee,[1] and not recognized by the Karaites, who only forbid heavy burdens. Jer. xvii. 22, 'Neither carry forth (*toẓi'u*) a burden out of your houses', shows that already in pre-exilic times it was specifically carrying into or out of a habitation which was considered sinful,[2] and the *Tĕ'ĕzāza Sanbat* explicitly mentions 'who takes something from his tent and brings something into it' (p. 20). In Jub. l. 8, 'whoever taketh up any burden to carry it out of his tent or out of his house', the influence of the Jeremiah passage is already discernible: although the tent is specified, it is evidently left to the reader to guess that taking in is equally forbidden. CDC xi. 7–8 leaves nothing to chance, but uses 'taking out' as a technical term: 'Let no man take out anything from the house outside or from the outside into the house.' The Mishnah (Shab. 1. 1) has a very similar technical term, including both transferring from inside to outside and vice versa: *yĕẓi'ah*, 'going out', which in itself

---

[1] Cf. Albeck, *Das Buch der Jubiläen und die Halacha*, p. 41.

[2] Cf. F. E. Laupheimer, 'Die außerpentateuchischen Quellen der Sabbatgesetze', in *Jahrb. d. Jüd.-Liter. Ges.* xxii (1931–2), 161–213.

makes little sense,[1] but appears to have been chosen in order to avoid the association with the Jeremiah passage, which might create the impression that the law was derived from an extra-pentateuchal source. In fact, later Jewish writers expended great ingenuity on discovering a pentateuchal source for this law, which according to the penalties threatened for its transgression (Tos. Shab. I. 3) was in Tannaitic times considered 'Biblical'. A thread of common school tradition runs from Jubilees via CDC to the Mishnah, but it is in CDC that it appears in its purest form.

A further school tradition which CDC shares with Rabbinic law is the specification of a temporary dwelling, about which some doubt might arise: 'Even if he be in a *sukkah* let him not take anything out of it or bring anything into it' (xii. 8–9). It is immaterial here whether *sukkah* means a booth for Tabernacles or a tent. In Rabbinic literature the only reference I know of is the problem of establishing an *'erub* in 'a city composed of tents', raised by Rab in P.T. Eru. v. I, 22c,[2] which in any case recognizes the special status of such an abode; one wonders whether it does not preserve some dim recollection of large temporary assemblies in the earlier period of Pharisaism.

Another case of this kind is that of the warning which in Rabbinic law must be administered by the witnesses *before* a capital crime is committed (M. San. 5. I). This is called *hathra'ah*, from the verb *hithrah*, which is doubtless[3] connected with Accad. *tarā'u*, 'to protect', Syr. *tarra'*, 'to educate', *tārā*, 'teacher'. The practice seems nowhere to be derived from a Biblical source.[4] In CDC ix. 3, 18, we find that a crime must be reported *bĕ-hokheah*, 'with

---

[1] Note, however, that in Gen. Rabba 26. 4 *yĕẓi'oth* is used for *hoẓa'oth*, 'expenses'.

[2] In the parallel, B.T. Eru. 55b, R. Huna speaks of 'hut dwellers'.

[3] The derivations proposed, from *torah* (Levy, Kohut) or *ra'ah* (Jastrow), are inherently improbable and grammatically difficult.

[4] The various Biblical derivations suggested B.T. San. 40b–41a are of the *asmakhta* type. The multiplicity of suggested derivations bears witness to the difficulty of finding a convincing one. Yet the language of B.T. Makk. 6b shows that it was taken for a Biblical injunction: 'R. Yose bar Judah (contemporary of Judah the Prince) says . . . because *hathra'ah* was only *given* to . . . .' The Biblical derivation is incorporated by Targ. Jon. into Num. xv. 33 (TJ's additions in brackets): 'And (the witnesses) that found him gathering sticks brought him (after they had warned him and he had continued to gather sticks) to Moses. . . .' See also *Tosafoth* ad loc.

reproof',[1] a phrase derived from Lev. xix. 17: 'Thou shalt surely
reprove thy neighbour.' The 'warning' is thus administered *after*
the crime. So, in fact, is the *hathra'ah* in the case of the rebellious
son (M. San. 8. 4), an archaic type of case in which, incidentally,
three witnesses are demanded, as in CDC ix.[2] The word *hokheaḥ*,
an infinitive used as a verbal noun, exists in the Mishnaic Hebrew
of the P.T. in two meanings: 'material evidence' (Nid. ii. 3, 50a—
in the parallel, B.T. Nid. 16b, *mokhiaḥ*) and 'a black mark against
someone' (twice in Demai ii. 1, 22c); it is even possible that in the
case of the shop that has sold forbidden goods for one day (loc.
cit.) the *hokheaḥ* consisted in an actual written record of the fact,
to be used whenever the offence was repeated, just as in CDC.
Here we have good reason to assume both a change of term and of
substance in Rabbinic practice: the change of terminology being
due, perhaps, to the feeling that *hokheaḥ* might be misunderstood
as 'evidence', this being the principal meaning of the verb in
Mishnaic Hebrew.

The extensive similarity in methods of analysis and presentation
and the almost complete difference in the actual words employed
call for an explanation. With only slight exaggeration we might
say that the Qumran and the Rabbinic terminologies are transla-
tions of each other. But which of these two is the original? Has the
Qumran sect recast the Mishnaic terminology into Biblical forms,
or does the Rabbinic terminology represent a Mishnaic Hebrew,
partly Aramaic, adaptation of legal language originally based on
that of the Pentateuch? This problem is not restricted to legal
terminology alone, but forms part of the wider question, why the
Qumran sect and Rabbinic Judaism used different forms of
Hebrew.[3]

[1] The rendering 'proof' (Hvidberg) is unlikely, since in Jewish law a witness
is not required to produce 'proof' apart from his statement. Even more decisive
is the variant *tokhaḥath* in DSD vi. 1, which can only mean 'reproof'.
[2] On this, see Epstein, *Mavo lĕ-nosaḥ ha-Mishnah*, p. 377. For other cases
where three witnesses are mentioned, cf. M. San. 3. 2; 5. 2.
[3] See pp. 67–69.

VIII

ISLAM AND THE QUMRAN SECT

LEST the theory that some late remnants of the Qumran sect survived in Arabia until the seventh century A.D. appear too fanciful from the outset, it is necessary to state that there are certain questions we must ask ourselves and to which the Scrolls themselves cannot provide the answer. These are:

1. What became of the sect after it left Qumran in what—judging by the abandonment of its library—seems to have been precipitate flight?[1]

2. On any dating of the sect, how can we explain that some of its teachings and terminology reappear in the last quarter of the first millennium? The theory of an earlier discovery of Cave No. I suffers from the fact that no such event is mentioned in the literature of the circles supposedly most deeply influenced.[2]

The probability that the suggestions made in the following pages are at least in part correct is enhanced by the circumstance that they deal not with major ideas—where independent origin in different places and 'mental climate' are complicating factors—but with small and secondary details, mainly of a philological nature. Since the latter are in many cases firmly anchored in a definite literary background, they can have been borrowed only by direct contact. They concern such matters as are admitted to be borrowed, even in the view of those scholars who believe Muhammad's religious ideas to have been largely original.[3]

The problem of the outside influences which went into the make-up of early Islam has attracted the attention of scholars ever since 1833, when Geiger published his youthful effort *Was hat Mohammed aus dem Judenthume aufgenommen?*[4] In 1867 Sprenger[5]

---

[1] It is hardly likely to have fled into Roman-occupied Judaea.
[2] No Jewish record exists of the discovery reported in the famous letter of Timotheus.   [3] e.g. Fück, *ZDMG* xc (1936), 509–25.
[4] Up-to-date bibliography in Katsh, *Judaism in Islam*, 1954.
[5] *Das Leben und die Lehre des Mohammed* (2nd edn., 1869).

demonstrated that much in Muhammad's religious outlook—including his theory of revelation and of his own prophetic office—cannot be explained on the basis of (Rabbinic) Jewish influence alone. Wellhausen[1] in 1887 coined the dictum: 'Von den Juden stammt nicht der Sauerteig, aber allerdings zum grossen Teile das Mehl, das später zugesetzt wurde.' In the present century T. Andrae[2] and K. Ahrens[3] made an attempt to show that much of the 'flour' was also Christian, while Torrey[4] brought to light much new material in support of Jewish origin, drawn especially from more intensive comparative study of the Koranic stories about O.T. prophets and Talmud and midrash.[5] In this connexion we may mention the effort of J. Finkel[6] to find the missing link in non-Rabbinic or pre-Rabbinic Jewish sects, and Gaster's[7] theory of Samaritan influence upon Muhammad. Amongst the partisans of Christian influence, too, there has been a tendency to seek the proximate source in Nestorianism or in Judaeo-Christian sects, such as the Ebionites,[8] Docetists, or Elkesaites.[9] The prominence of Gnostic traits in Islam moved C. Clemens[10] in 1921 to ascribe to Manichaeism a decisive influence upon it.

[1] *Reste arabischen Heidentums*, 2nd edn. (1927), p. 242.
[2] *Der Ursprung des Islams und das Christentum*, 1926.
[3] 'Christliches im Quran', *ZDMG* lxxxiv (1930), 15–68, 148–90.
[4] *Jewish Foundations of Islam*, 1933.
[5] The possibilities of this are by no means exhausted; see, e.g., Yahuda, *Goldziher Memorial Volume*, i (1948), 280–308, who brings further elucidation from recently-published Yemenite midrashim. We may add that Haman's presence at Pharaoh's court (by identification with his ancestor Amalek, who is in the midrash one of Pharaoh's advisers) may be alluded to in Alkabez's *Měnoth ha-Levi* (Venice, 1585, f. 153b), which says Haman found one of the treasures buried by Joseph. Joseph's vision of the *burhān* (Ethiopic = 'light') of his Lord (12. 24) may connect with the late midrash where God threatens Joseph that He will cast away the *Even Shěthiyyah* and reduce the world to Chaos (Ginzberg, *Legends*, ii. 54)—the *Even Shěthiyyah* being the source of the first light at the Creation (ibid. i. 12).
[6] 'Old-Israelitish Tradition in the Koran', *PAAJR* ii (1931), 7–21; 'Jewish, Christian and Samaritan Influences on Arabia', *D. B. Macdonald Presentation Volume* (1933), pp. 147–66.
[7] 'Samaritans', in *Enc. Isl.* iv. 124–9.
[8] Whose identity with the Qumran sect has been advocated by J. L. Teicher.
[9] On this group, who have some points of contact with the Qumran sect, see Waitz, in *Harnack-Ehrung* (1921), pp. 87–104; Brandt in *Enc. Rel. and Ethics*, s.v.; Cullmann, *Le probl. littér. et hist. du roman pseudo-clémentin* (1930), pp. 170–83.
[10] In *Harnack-Ehrung* (1921), pp. 249–62.

In view of this inconclusive search it seems not unreasonable to test also possible connexions with the Qumran sect, especially as the latter lies at the intersection of almost all the previous lines of inquiry: it has close contact both with Rabbinic and non-Rabbinic Judaism, shows certain Gnostic traits,[1] and has numerous connections both with the early Church and the Judaeo-Christian sects. Thus features common to it, Islam, and one of the foregoing can provide further support for a connexion between it and Islam, provided such a connexion has been made probable by traits common to the Qumran sect and Islam alone.

The possibility of the main Jewish influence on Muhammad having been that of a heretical Jewish sect was first put forward by S. D. Goitein in 1933,[2] and elaborated in 1953,[3] when he specified this sect as one 'strongly influenced by Christianity'. In his Columbia University lectures of the same year,[4] he suggested that Muhammad was in his debate with the Jews of Medina merely carrying on an internal Jewish controversy, being supplied with arguments by his heretical teachers,[5] and also seriously weighed the possibility of these teachers coming from 'an offshoot of the community of the Dead Sea Scrolls',[6] but rejected this, 'because if it were so, it would not have had such close affinities with the Talmudic literature to which the Koran bears such eloquent testimony'.

By stressing the close affinities of the Qumran sect with Rabbinic Judaism, the preceding pages have endeavoured to remove just that objection. I may now set out in detail the similarities which I have so far encountered, and then try to assess their significance.

1. Like the Qumran literature, the Koran makes extensive use of the symbolism of light and darkness to distinguish between the realms of God and Satan, e.g. 'Allah is the light of heavens and earth . . . Allah guides to His light whom He wills . . . as to those

---

[1] Cf. B. Reicke, *N.T. Studies*, i (1954) 137–41.

[2] In a lecture delivered at Tel-Aviv.

[3] *Gotthold Weil Jubilee Volume* (1952), pp. 10–23 (in Hebrew).

[4] Published in the *Jewish Observer*, 1953–4; now as *Jews and Arabs* (New York, 1955).

[5] *Jewish Observer* of 5 Dec. 1952, p. 12.

[6] Ibid., 28 Nov. 1952, p. 12; *Jews and Arabs*, pp. 57–58.

who disbelieve, their deeds are like . . . darkness upon a vast
abysmal sea, layer upon layer of darkness . . . and he for whom
Allah has not appointed light, for him there is no light' (24. 35-40).
This symbolism, of course, also exists in the N.T., which even has
the Qumran term 'children of light',[1] missing in the Koran, but
does not, like Qumran literature and the Koran, link 'light' with
the idea of absolute predestination (cf. Eph. v. 8, 'ye were darkness
before, but now ye are light in the Lord'). The Koran also frequently repeats the idea that Allah misleads the sinners, for which
cf. CDC ii. 13, 'but those whom He hated, He misled'.

2. The leader of the sons of light is the 'prince of lights',[2] and
it is he by whose hand Moses and Aaron were raised, while Belial
raised Jannes and Mambres (CDC v. 18). Similarly, Muhammad's
career is guided by Gabriel, called 'the holy spirit' in 16. 104;
26. 193. Gabriel is the 'herald of light'[3] in the apocryphal *Story of
Joseph the Carpenter*.[4] In DSW, on the other hand, Michael is the
special angel appointed over Israel. Yadin[2] argues from this and
other sources that in fact Michael was the prince of lights; however, the very passage he adduces, DSW xvii. 6-8, can also be
taken as an argument against it. If, as is said there, 'God made
mighty (*he'ĕdhir*) the office of Michael with light of eternities . . .
so as to raise amongst the angels the office of Michael and the
authority of Israel amongst all flesh', this implies that Michael's
power—like that of Israel—is for the time being in eclipse, and
that the 'light' will only be bestowed upon him at the final battle.
A certain rivalry between Michael and Gabriel is implied by the
tradition, preserved in the Ethiopic poem *Ṭabība Ṭabībān*,[5] that
'Gabriel was raised like Michael' after the fall of Lucifer. However, it must be noted that the name of Gabriel for the guiding
angel appears only at Medina, and that an Islamic tradition[6] tells
us that the Jews of Medina held Gabriel to be the angel of divine
wrath. The name may thus be secondary and polemical,[7] and the

---

[1] Luke xvi. 8; John xii. 36; Eph. v. 8; 1 Thess. v. 5.
[2] Cf. Yadin, ch. 9, para. 5.   [3] For 'herald' = teacher, cf. pp. 55, 98.
[4] Ch. xxii. This apocryphal Gospel exists in Arabic.
[5] Dillmann, *Chrestomathia Aethiopica*, p. 108, vs. 3, line 2.
[6] See Katsh, op. cit., pp. 68-69.
[7] Cf. also O'Shaughnessy, *The Development of the Meaning of Spirit in the
Qur'an* (1953), pp. 48-49.

connexion with Qumran thought, while attractive, remains obscure.

3. Like the Qumran sect and the N.T., Muhammad held the entire O.T., prophets and all, to be books of prediction.[1] They were indeed thought also in Rabbinic literature to predict details of the Messianic coming, so that the difference lies not so much in the attitude to the O.T. as in the evaluation of one's own time, which the former three identified with that preceding the Coming. Muhammad did not get his belief, that his coming and actions were foretold in the 'Torah', from Christian sources, since he tells us himself: 'And lo, it is in the scriptures of the men of old. Is it not a sign for them that the learned ones of the children of Israel know it?' (26. 197). Moses is made to say: 'I shall write down my mercy for those that believe in my verses, that follow the gentile prophet whom they shall find written down for them in the Torah and the Gospel'[2] (7. 156–7). Details of his ministry were foretold, as, for example, the change of the direction of prayer: 'Those unto whom we gave the scripture know this as they know their sons, but a party of them knowingly conceal the truth' (2. 146).

This kind of prediction was expected from Jews. Ṭabarī[3] tells how Kaʿb al-Aḥbār informed ʿOmar I that he had read in the Torah of his impending death. To the latter's question, 'Did you really find ʿOmar b. al-Khaṭṭāb in the Torah?', he replies, 'Not your name, but your description and appearance'. Similarly, Kaʿb's son predicted the death of ʿAmr b. Saʿīd, and later an exilarch the death of Ḥusain.[4] We are reminded of Josephus' statement about the Essenes (BJ II. viii. 12): 'There are some among them who profess to foretell the future, being versed from their early years in holy books, &c.'[5] It is hardly an activity typical of Rabbinic Jewry, but this kind of lower prophecy must have been widespread amongst the Qumran sect, to judge from the treatise on physiognomy preserved amongst the fragments from Cave IV.

[1] Cf. below, p. 128, on the *Pesher* to Psalms.

[2] Since Waraqa also had a 'gospel' in Hebrew, it is not impossible that the 'gospel' (*injīl*) in this connexion refers to a sectarian writing rather than the N.T.

[3] Leiden edn., i. 5, pp. 2722–3.

[4] Cf. Van Vloten, *Recherches sur la domination arabe* (1894), pp. 55–56.

[5] See also Thackeray's note in the Loeb edn., and cf. the instance in *Ant.* xv. x. 5.

3. The use of the O.T. for prognosis is, of course, called *pesher* by the Qumran sect, with the verb *pashar* Qal (לפשור, DSH ii. 8). The noun occurs Eccles. viii. 1, not in any technical sense, and both noun and verb in Bibl. Aram., in Samar., and in Syr. for the interpretation of dreams. For the technical sense of interpretation Bacher[1] has no Tannaitic example and only one from the *Pesiqta*. Otherwise, Rabbinic Hebrew uses *prsh* Pi'el. The use of *pshr* seems ultimately to be derived from Accadian *pašāru*, 'to interpret a dream', *pišīru*, 'interpretation', but the application to the interpretation of texts seems to have arisen in the special circumstances of the Qumran sect, where such interpretation was a form of inspiration. It is therefore significant when we find in Koran 25. 32 (second Meccan period) the verbal noun *tafsīr* in a context referring to sacred books,[2] and in Islamic usage *fassara* as the normal word for Koran interpretation.

4. We learn from various sources about the pre-Islamic *ḥanīfs*, men who had accepted monotheism without becoming Jews or Christians[3] and practised asceticism. The Koran uses this term six times of Abraham, twice of Muhammad (10. 105; 30. 29), and twice of the Muslim community (22. 32; 98. 4). The word has so far defied interpretation.[4] It is different in form from Syr. *ḥanpā*, 'heathen', with which it is most frequently connected, but fairly close to Heb. *ḥānēf*, which in MH means one who is insincere in his faith.[5] By connecting it either with the Syriac or the MH word, we imply that it was a name given to these men by Jews or Christians and misunderstood by them as a name of honour.

It is, however, possible to suggest an explanation which makes *ḥanīf* a straightforward descriptive word. The Qumran sect had proselytes among its ranks (*gerim*, CDC xiv. 6); in DSD v. 6 these are called *ha-nilwim 'ălehem*, 'they that join themselves unto them'.[6] Arabic *ḥanafa*, 'to incline, turn', is a synonym of Arab.

---

[1] *Die exegetische Terminologie* (1905), ii. 174.
[2] See also Jeffery, *The Foreign Vocabulary of the Qur'an* (Baroda, 1938), p. 92.
[3] There were also full proselytes to Judaism; cf. Nöldeke, *ZDMG* xli (1887), 720.
[4] The various suggestions are summarized in Hirschberg, *Jüdische und christliche Lehren im vor- und frühislamischen Arabien* (Krakow, 1939), p. 33, n. 1.
[5] Gen. Rabba 25. 1: 'Enoch was a *ḥanef*, being at times righteous, at others wicked'; cf. also *ḥănefē Torah*, B.T. Soṭ. 42a.
[6] Used for 'proselyte' in Isa. xiv. 1; lvi. 3, 6; Zech. ii. 15.

lawā; the Hebrew word may thus, not unreasonably, have been understood from its Arabic homonym as 'those who incline', viz. towards the teaching of the sect.

Since the Qumran sect daily expected the Messianic coming, there was not much point in proselytizing unless the heathen proselytes played some role in its plan of salvation. The connexion of the hanif movement with the sect thus gains ground from what we shall learn later of the attitude to the 'gentile prophet'.

5. Wellhausen's chief objection[1] to a Jewish origin of Islam was its intense preoccupation with the end of the world, which is absent in Talmudic Judaism, and, as Wellhausen admits, also from seventh-century Christianity. It remained a preoccupation of Muslims until *c.* A.D. 750, when those interested in learning in Egypt are said to have studied nothing but eschatological prophecies.[2] All its eschatological terminology must therefore be early.[3] It is mostly attached to the name of Ka'b al-Aḥbār. Kuthayyir 'Azza (d. A.D. 723) says:

That is the Mahdī of whom Ka'b the fellow of the *aḥbār* told us in times past.[4]

As we know, intense Messianism was also one of the characteristics of the Qumran sect. It is important that precisely in the field of eschatological terminology connexions exist.

6. The generic Muslim name for Messianic events is *malḥama*, pl. *malāḥim*.[5] This is obviously the Hebrew word *milḥamah*, 'war', but in Rabbinic parlance these events are called *ḥevlē ha-Mashiaḥ*, 'birth pangs of the Messiah', and the only place, to my knowledge, where *milḥamah* occurs in this sense is in a report about the finding of an old Messianic scroll, B.T. San. 97b. In DSW the word occurs in the Messianic sense in the title, and again in 'the epochs of the wars of Thine hands', xi. 8. While the Messianic wars in Rabbinic eschatology are fought out by the heathen nations, the war of DSW is fought by Israel, begins in the 'desert of Jerusalem', and ends

---

[1] *Reste arabischen Heidentums*, 2nd edn. (1927), pp. 240–2.
[2] Nawawī, *Tahdhīb*, xi. 319; cf. Goldziher, *Muhammedanische Studien*, ii. 73.
[3] Cf. Casanova, *Mohammed et la fin du monde* (1911), *passim*.
[4] Mas'ūdī, *Prairies d'Or*, v. 181.
[5] On which see Steinschneider, *ZDMG* xxviii (1874), 627–59; Goldziher, *Muhammedanische Studien*, ii. 73, 127.

forty years later with the conquest of Ham and Japheth.[1] The Muslim *malḥama* begins at Medina and ends with the destruction of 'Rome' (Constantinople),[2] according to one version by 70,000 'sons of Isaac'.[3] Probably the final event of the sectarian war also was the conquest of Rome.

It is interesting to note, in this connexion, that Saadiah renders *ish milḥamah* in Exod. xv. 3 as *dhū 'l-malāḥim*, apparently following the eschatological interpretation of the song hinted at in B.T. San. 91b.

7. One of the stages of the *malḥama* is called *al-harj*, a word without any meaning in Arabic,[4] but evidently the Hebrew *heregh*, 'slaughter'. This occurs in DST xv. 17, *yom hăreghah*. The latter is borrowed from Jer. xii. 3, but the Arabic form reminds one more of *heregh* in Isa. xxx. 25, 'on the day of the great slaughter, when the towers fall'.

8. The word *ḥashr* occurs twice in the Koran, once in the early Sura 55. 44, in an eschatological setting, and again in the Medinean 59. 2, in connexion with the destruction of the Jewish Banū Naḍīr. There is, of course, the common Koranic verb *ḥashara*, 'to gather',[5] and the sense 'gathering' fits the context in the first passage. In the second there is no 'gathering', and Muslim commentators find much difficulty in accounting for the word. It is just possible that we may have here, perhaps used sneeringly, the word *naḥshīr* which describes the final battle in DSW i. 9, 10, 13. This word, ultimately from Persian *nakhchīr*, 'hunt', occurs also in Syriac and in the derivation *naḥshīrkhān*, 'hunter', in Targumic Aramaic.[6] In Syriac it appears once as *ḥashīrā*,[7] which

---

[1] The Banū Qantūrā', a Turkish people, play a part in Muslim eschatology; cf. Attema, *De mohammedaansche opvattingen omtrent het tijdstip van den jongsten dag en zijn voorteekenen* (1942), p. 57. In DSW ii. 13 the Benē Qĕṭurah are the last Semitic people to be conquered.

[2] Cf. Attema, op. cit., pp. 89 seq. (Ibn Ḥanbal, ii. 174; vi. 27, &c.).

[3] Ibid., pp. 92–93 (Muslim 52. 79). For the number, cf. in DSW: seven skirmishing standards, seven heavy infantry formations, &c., and the 'myriad' as the largest military unit.

[4] For occurrences, see Attema, pp. 63–66. Ibn Ḥanbal, v. 389, says the word is Ethiopic: there is no such word in Ethiopic, but it is used in South-Arabian.

[5] South-Arabian *ḥśr* (note the sibilant), 'to collect produce', perhaps MH *ḥshr*, 'to distil (?)'.   [6] See Yadin ad. loc.

[7] Cf. Brockelmann, *Lexicon*, 2nd edn., p. 263b.

is possibly not a scribal error, but due to the *na-* being taken as a nominal prefix.[1] The matter, however, is rather uncertain.

9. The name of the Muslim Messiah, *mahdī*, literally 'the rightly guided one', is strange.[2] It is 'written of him in the *Malāḥim* books that he will fill the earth with justice'.[3] The preoccupation with justice which dominates Hebrew prophecy is alien to Islam, and its appearance in this connexion unusual. Perhaps we have here some attempt at translating *moreh ha-ẓedheq*. We instinctively take this as an active participle, but it is not at all impossible to read *mureh ha-ẓedheq*, 'he that is taught righteousness', stressing the inspirational side of his character.[4]

10. We are on safer ground with the Arabic name for the Antichrist (and also occasionally for the devil), *dajjāl*. This is said to be a loan from Syriac *daggālā*, which (like the corresponding Chr. Pal. Aram. word) means indeed 'liar', but not 'Antichrist', which is *měshīḥā dě-dhaggālūthā*. In the scrolls the opponent of the Teacher of Righteousness is called the teacher (or man) of lies,[5] the latter form borrowed from Prov. xix. 22. Now the root *dgl*, 'to lie', appears only in the Syriacizing Targum to Proverbs (mostly corrupted to *rgl*). In xix. 22 we have, indeed, *gavrā kaddāvā* (though Pesh. has *gavrā da-mdaggel*), but a few verses farther on we get *daggalā* as translation of *běliyaʿal* (in 'a false witness', Pesh. ʿāwālā). The transition from 'liar' to 'Antichrist' thus seems to have taken place in a Jewish milieu rather than in a Christian one, and it might at least be surmised that it served as an Aramaic rendering for *ish kazav*. Incidentally, *dajjāl* also appears in Muslim eschatology simply as 'false teacher', as in the tradition of the thirty *dajjālūn*, where another version has thirty *kadhdhābūn*.[6]

11. The other name for the devil, *Iblīs*, is generally derived

---

[1] As, e.g., in *nabrīḥā=barḥā*, 'he-goat'.   [2] Cf. Casanova, op. cit., pp. 66–67.
[3] Bīrūnī, tr. Sachau, p. 19. The idea also in traditions (B. Ḥanbal, iii. 36; A. Dāʾūd, 35:1, No. 3), cf. Attema, p. 101.
[4] Since the name is based on Hos. x. 12, where the subject of 'will teach' is God, a passive sense is perhaps more faithful to Scripture. Pesh. and Vulg., however, have the active participle.
[5] See above, p. 55.
[6] Attema, p. 53. Muhammad is said to have called a Jew in Medina *dajjāl* (Van Vloten, op. cit., p. 59): does this perhaps mean that Muhammad's Jewish friends called that man 'teacher of lies'?

from διάβολος, and it has been suggested that the d- was dropped owing to its being taken as the Syriac genitive particle. Jeffery[1] rightly points out that the name was not current in Syriac. We might therefore draw attention to the theory of Künstlinger[2] and J. Finkel,[3] according to which the name was corrupted from a hypothetical *Belias*; cf. the *Beliar* of some Greek pseudepigrapha. This would establish a further connexion with the scrolls, where Belial frequently occurs as the name of the 'prince of darkness'.

12. The sinners, who hide the proofs and the revelation received by them, shall be cursed by Allah and 'those who curse' (2. 159); those who die in unbelief have upon them the curse of 'Allah and the angels and all men'. Similarly, in CDC xx. 8 the backslider will be cursed by 'all the holy ones (= angels) of the highmost'.[4]

13. Aḥmad b. Muḥammad ath-Thaʿlabī (d. A.D. 1035) in his *Stories of the Prophets*[5] says that the name of Muhammad was created 2,000 years before the creation of the world and inscribed on the throne of glory. This is remarkably like the midrashic statement about the name of the Messiah having been created before the world (Gen. Rabba 1. 4); even closer is the version in the late Midr. Psalms on Ps. xc, in which all the pre-existing things were created 2,000 years[6] before the world and the name of the Messiah is engraved on the altar of the heavenly sanctuary. In CDC the names of the elect are fixed from all eternity (CDC ii. 13; iv. 5). Similarly, Koran 30. 56 states: 'And to those to whom knowledge and faith have been given, say, you are permanently inscribed in the book of Allah until the day of the resurrection.'[7] The Shiʿite messiah must bear the same pre-created name as Muhammad.[8]

---

[1] *The Foreign Vocabulary of the Qur'an*, p. 48.
[2] *Rocznik Orient.* iv (1928), 238–47.
[3] *D. B. Macdonald Presentation Volume*, p. 156.
[4] Perhaps the 'cursers' are none but the 'angels of destruction'; CDC ii. 6; DSW xiii. 12.   [5] Cairo edn., p. 181.
[6] The number is in the midrash based on *yom yom* in Prov. viii. 31 (one day of God = 1,000 years), hence no doubt the Jewish version is the original one.
[7] Jeffery, *The Qur'an as Scripture* (1952), p. 10, rightly takes this to mean that the names were inscribed; the interpretation of the Muslim commentators is different.   [8] Casanova, op. cit., p. 64.

14. An important difference between the Scrolls and Rabbinic Judaism is that the latter knows of an evil force within man, the 'evil inclination',[1] while the Qumran sect, like Christianity, the Mandaeans, and some late midrashim (*Pirqe R. Eliezer, Midrash ha-Gadol*),[2] know only of an external Satan who misleads men into sin. This, of course, is the position of Islam, too. Possibly a polemic against the doctrine of the internal duality in man is reflected in the statement, Koran 33. 4, in the wake of a rather obscure reference to divorce and adoption, 'Allah has not given man two hearts.'

The above items are not all of the same value; on the other hand, it seems not unlikely that the number of correspondences could be increased. Their importance, as I have said before, rests precisely on their comparative unimportance, which makes independent creation in most of the cases rather improbable. We must now attempt to trace the way in which they may have reached Muhammad.

His contemporaries were aware that he had informants, and called his teachings 'ancient fables which he has written from dictation in the morning and in the evening' (25. 4). The prophet admitted this indirectly when he said: 'the speech of him at whom they hint is barbaric,[3] but this Koran is clear Arabic speech' (16. 103). Tradition tells us that Muhammad did not understand the meaning and nature of his visions, and had to be enlightened by the Judaizing cousin of his wife, Waraqa;[4] the latter was in possession of a 'gospel' which he had copied in Hebrew.[5] The presence of informants is also indicated by the fact that Biblical examples are completely missing from the earliest Suras[6] and during the first Meccan period are stated with cryptic brevity smacking of unfamiliarity.[7] But these teachers did not only tell

---

[1] Although the story of the slaughtering of the 'evil inclination' (B.T. Suk. 52a) suggests that it could also be imagined as a person.

[2] Hirschberg, op. cit., p. 52.

[3] This may either mean foreign, or Arabic badly pronounced.

[4] Blachère, *Le problème de Mahomet* (1952), p. 41.

[5] Bukhārī, ed. Krehl, i. 5.

[6] In fact, historical examples are not used at all before Sura 105; cf. Attema, op. cit., p. 9, n. 8.

[7] e.g. (in the order of Suras as in Nöldeke) 87. 19; 95. 2; 85. 18; 73. 15; 53. 52. The earliest of these, 87. 19, refers to the 'scrolls of Abraham and Moses';

him Biblical stories: like Waraqa, they also enlightened him about his own mission.

Muhammad uses of himself the phrase *an-nabī al-ummī*,[1] which has long been recognized to mean 'the gentile prophet', derived from the MH *ummoth ha-ʿolam*, 'gentes mundi',[2] and not, as the Muslim commentators say, 'the illiterate prophet'. In 62. 2 this is expressed even more clearly as 'the prophet raised up from the midst of the gentiles (*ummiyyūna*)'. The word occurs only in connexion with prophecy: it is therefore likely that he received the whole phrase from a Jewish source. What does 'gentile prophet' mean?

The Byzantine chronicler, Theophanes,[3] writing about A.D. 815, relates that certain prominent Jews believed Muhammad to be the Messiah they expected. They went to him, but soon realized their hopes were false, nevertheless they stayed on and managed to turn him against the Christians. The same story is also preserved in a Jewish account from the Genizah.[4] This claims that their conversion was feigned, and their plan was to prevent him from turning against the Jews. Also some of their names are given. The most important one is the famous Kaʿb al-Aḥbār,[5] to whom so many of the Biblical and eschatological items in Arabic tradition are traced back. B. Chapira[6] has made it probable that writings by him continued to circulate amongst orthodox Jews. His title is suggestive: although later Muslim writers say *aḥbār* is a singular and means 'Rabbi', its form is obviously a plural of *ḥaber*, and he is called 'Kaʿb of the *ḥaberim*'; this was still clear to Kuthayyir ʿAzza[7] when he called him 'the fellow of the *aḥbār*'. However, *ḥaber* was not a common title of a Rabbi in the seventh century, and it may show him to have belonged to a group where the title was still typical.

Whether the story of these converts is true or not—and it is

this almost gives the impression as if this was written under the impetus of some new source with which he had just become acquainted.

[1] 7. 157–8.
[2] Jeffery, *Foreign Vocabulary*, p. 69, recognizes *umma* as a loan-word, but does not discuss *ummī*.
[3] i. 333; cf. Schwabe, *Tarbiz*, ii (1930–1), 74 seq.
[4] Ed. Leveen, *JQR* xvi (1925–6), 399–406; cf. Baneth, *Tarbiz*, iii (1931–2), 112–16.
[5] On him, cf. M. Perlmann, *Joshua Starr Memorial Volume* (1953), pp. 85–99; *JQR* xlv (1954), 48–58.
[6] *RÉJ* lxix (1919), 86–107.   [7] In the verse quoted above, p. 118.

difficult to see why Jews should have circulated it—the conversion of Ka'b is undoubtedly an historical fact. What could have caused a man of such learning to become a convert and Muslim propagandist? I think the answer can be found in Sura 7. 156–8 (Medinean): 'the gentile prophet whom ye find written in the Torah . . . and who will remove from them their burden and the fetters that are upon them'. The Jews of Arabia were free and prosperous; the 'fetters' clearly point to a Byzantine origin of the idea. Whoever communicated the thought to Muhammad must have seen in him a possible liberator of Jewry from the yoke of the 'kingdoms', a figure in the Messianic drama.

This view is put unequivocally in the 'Secrets revealed to R. Simeon bar Yoḥai',[1] which date, as has been shown by B. Lewis,[2] from the end of the Omayyad dynasty c. A.D. 750 and probably contain a nucleus written at the very beginning of the Islamic conquests. We read there: 'Metatron answered and said, God only raises the kingdom of Ishmael to save you from this wicked power,[3] and He will establish over them a prophet according to His desire (navi ki-rĕẓono).'[4] Ibn Hishām, indeed, tells us[5] that the Jews of Medina expected such a prophet just before Muhammad appeared on the scene. There seems to have been some Messianic ferment leading to difficulties. Balādhurī[6] has preserved the information that at the time some Jewish merchants lived at Ṭā'if, who had been banished (ṭuridū) from Yemen and Yathrib (i.e. Medina). While Yemenites might, as Lammens suggested,[7] have come there after the destruction of the Jewish kingdom in Yemen, Jews from Medina can have been 'banished' only as a result of internal quarrels. It is suggestive that Ṭā'if was the home town of the Ḥanīf poet Umayya ibn Abī 'ṣ-Ṣalt, whose work exhibits such curious similarity with the Koran.[8]

[1] Publ. Jellinek, Beth ha-Midrasch, iii (1855), 78–82.
[2] 'An Apocalyptic Vision of Islamic History', BSOAS xiii (1950), 308–38.
[3] The common appellation of the Roman Empire, both in the Scrolls and in Rabbinic literature. Cf. CDC vi. 10; DSW i. 13; B.T. Shab. 15a: '180 years before the Temple was destroyed, the wicked kingdom atacked Israel.'
[4] The phrase 'according to His desire' for God's cosmic plan occurs also DSD v. 1, as well as in the Kaddish prayer (ki-rĕʿutheh).
[5] i. 286, 373; cf. Pautz, Muhammed's Lehre von der Offenbarung (1898), p. 130.
[6] Futūḥ, Leiden edn., p. 56.   [7] Ta'if, p. 88.
[8] On him, see Hirschberg, op. cit.

The attitude of certain Jews to Muhammad's revelations is shown by two passages in Suras from the end of the Meccan period: 'when the Koran is being recited to them they say, We believe in it, it is the truth from our Lord' (28. 53); 'those unto whom we gave the scriptures rejoice in what has been revealed to thee, but of the (Arab) tribes there are who deny some of it' (13. 36). Yet when Muhammad came to Medina he met with the undisguised hostility and ridicule of the Jewish community there. This becomes much easier to understand if we assume that the teachings he brought were not unfamiliar to the Medinean Jews, being those of heretics they had but recently expelled. But above all, the theory of heretical Jewish mentors explains the remarkable knowledge Muhammad soon displays of inner-Jewish controversies and his use of subtle points of Jewish theology, and even of Hebrew phrases, in his debate with the Medinean Jews.

Thus he attacks them for being insufficiently concerned with the impending judgement day: 'if the abode of the world-to-come with God were reserved to you to the exclusion of all other men, then, if ye were speaking the truth, ye should long for death' (2. 94). This is aimed at the doctrine of M. San. 10. 1, 'All Israel have a share in the world-to-come.'[1] Even more specific: the *ummiyyūna* among the Jews[2] believe that 'hell-fire will not touch us save for some days' (2. 79)—a reference to the teaching of R. Akiba, who limits a Jew's stay in Gehenna to twelve months, and of his contemporary Johanan b. Nuri, who thought it to be seven days only (M. Edu. 2. 10).

After having repeated the midrashic statement that the Jews accepted the Torah only after Mount Sinai had been held threateningly over their heads,[3] he goes on to say (2. 93) that instead of the expected 'we hear and obey' they said *sami'nā wa-'aṣīnā*, thus 'changing the words from their proper places'. As Obermann[4] has shown, these words, in Arabic 'we hear and disobey', are in fact

---

[1] Except heretics. It is a piquant thought that Muhammad's mentors made him here argue their own private cause.

[2] Here *ummiyyūna* probably = Am-Haareẓ; cf. Horovitz, *HUCA* ii (1925), 191.

[3] Cf. Ginzberg, *Legends*, iii. 92.

[4] 'Koran and Aggada: The Events at Mount Sinai', *AJSLL* lviii (1941), 23–48, especially 41–44.

the *shamaʻnu wĕ-ʻaśinu* of Deut. v. 24, as against the *naʻăśeh wĕ-nishmaʻ* of Exod. xxiv. 7. We have Talmudic authority that this difference in Scripture was the subject of sectarian attacks against the Rabbis.[1]

We can now understand why so many of Muhammad's attacks against the Jews of Medina can be paralleled from the New Testament:[2] both the N.T. and he drew from the same sectarian arsenal. Thus the Jews are frequently accused of slaying the prophets wrongfully.[3] This, of course, also occurs in the N.T. (Matt. v. 12; xxiii. 31), but CDC vii. 18 already accuses the Jews of despising the words of the prophets; cf. also Test. Levi xvi. 2. We may thus have a development of the Qumran view. Indeed, such arguments in both N.T. and Koran may have preserved much which by accident has not been preserved amongst the fragments of the Qumran literature available to us.

In a number of passages Muhammad holds up his own Jewish partisans as an example to the Medinean Jews. We may expect to learn from these something of their identity. That they were Jews is evident from 3. 110: 'Ye were the best community that has been put forth to mankind, enjoining right conduct and forbidding what is wrong and believing in Allah. If the people of the book believed, it would be better for them, but some of them are believers and most are evildoers.' We thus learn that the 'believers' were few in comparison with the mass of the Jews, and that the difference was not merely in whether they believed in Muhammad or not, but was halakhic. What it was, we learn further from 10. 93; 45. 17: the Jews 'did not differ until the knowledge came to them'. While other groups always claimed to preserve the pristine purity of Judaism, the Qumran sect ascribed its halakhah to the new revelation of 'hidden things concerning which all Israel had gone astray' (CDC iii. 13). It is those Jews who 'have the knowledge' who accept Muhammad's claims (17. 108), saying, 'the promise of our

[1] B.T. Shab. 88a; Ket. 112a; in most copies 'Sadducee' replaces 'Min', because of the censorship (which always insisted that 'Min' meant a Christian).

[2] Cf. Ahrens, *ZDMG* lxxxiv (1930), 156–9; Andrae, *Der Ursprung des Islam und das Christentum*, pp. 198 seq.

[3] 2. 58, 81, 85; 3. 20, 112, 177, 180; 4. 154; 5. 74. For 'wrongfully' (*bi-ghairi ḥaqqin*), cf. *ăsher lo bĕ-mishpaṭ*, DSD vii. 13.

Lord is indeed carried out'—i.e. Muhammad is the 'gentile prophet' expected. The 'differing' is about the interpretation of scripture (11. 110; 41. 45); only a 'group' (*farīq*) distorts scripture (3. 78; 4. 45). The distorters of scripture in CDC i. 18–19 are chided in words based on Isa. xxx. 10 for speaking *ḥălaqoth*, 'smooth things', which is an abbreviation of the idiom exhibited in *maḥăliq lěshono*, Prov. xxviii. 43, where Saadiah translates *al-mulayyinu lahu lisānahu*. The way of speaking of the wicked *farīq* is in Koran 3. 78 expressed by the words *yalwūna* (written يلون) *alsinatahum bil-kitābi*, 'they make their tongues involved concerning the book': possibly we have here an Arabic popular etymology (or merely a misreading?) of the Hebrew phrase.

As against these, there is 'among you a community (*umma*) that calls to that which is right' (3. 107); 'and of the people of Moses there is a community who guide rightly (or are rightly guided) with truth and thereby become just' (7. 159); 'They are not the same as a community among the people of the book who stand and read the verses of God part of the night, while prostrating them-selves, who believe in God and in the last day . . . they are the upright' (3. 113). In the last quotation we may well have an allusion to the practice of studying one third of all the nights,[1] according to DSD vi. 7 combined with communal prayer. The name, 'the upright' (*aṣ-ṣāliḥūna*), reminds one that the Hebrew equivalent, *yěsharim*, appears practically as a name of the Qumran sect.[2]

It may well be that sectarian writings account for the 'scrolls of Abraham and Moses', from which Muhammad quotes in the early Sura 53. 36–54, for Waraqa's 'gospel', and for the 'book of the Jews' which Zaid, at Muhammad's order, 'studied within two weeks'.[3] From such books may have come the lists of moral precepts (2. 176) or the rewritings of the Decalogue in 17. 23–40 (second Meccan period) and 6. 152 seq. (third Meccan period). Finally, this may account for the curious information of Thaʿlabī[4]

---

[1] Cf. p. 43.

[2] CDC xx. 2; DSD iii. 1; iv. 22. Ibn Quṭaiba relates that before Muhammad's mission *zindīqs* were making proselytes at Mecca (cf. Obermann, in *The Arab Heritage*, Princeton, 1944, p. 60). In later Arabic *zindīq* means Gnostic. It prob-ably comes from Syriac *zaddīqā*, 'upright', hence it is just possible we have here another reference to the *yěsharim*. [3] A. Dāʾūd, ii. 34; Balādhurī, *Futūḥ*, p. 477.

[4] *Qiṣaṣ al-anbiyāʾ*, Cairo edn., p. 244.

that of the Psalms 50 dealt with ethical matters, 50 were prophecies concerning the first exile, and 50 dealt with the Roman oppression. Did his informants know about a *Pesher* on Psalms?

To sum up, there can be little doubt that Muhammad had Jewish contacts before coming to Medina; it is highly probable that they were heretical, anti-Rabbinic Jews; and a number of terminological and ideological details suggest the Qumran sect.

Arabia was the obvious place for a group from the neighbourhood of the Dead Sea to flee to. The desert regions of Transjordan and the northern Hijaz were the home of several Judaeo-Christian sects, and 'Arabia' was known to the Church Fathers to be *ferax haereseon*. With the Qumran sect, the exodus into the desert may have been part of their Messianic plan. DSD viii. 13 speaks of the going into the desert as an event of the Messianic future; DSW i. 2–3 envisages the return of the 'exiles of the desert' 'from the desert of the nations'. As Khirbet Qumran lies within the confines of the Promised Land, the very term 'desert of the nations' suggests an exodus into Arabia. On the other hand, they were not the only Jews in the Peninsula. There was the large community of the Yemen, and the village dwellers of the Wādī 'l-Qurā, as well as the prominently Aaronid[1] city of Medina. These were Rabbinic Jews, and relations could hardly have been good. Or possibly the main body stayed in eastern Transjordan, the region through which Muhammad travelled as a young man, and where he is said to have met the 'monk'[2] Baḥīra,[3] who recognized him from a mark on his body as the future prophet; again a method reminding us of the Qumran fragments on physiognomy.

If our theory is right, it will go a long way towards explaining how certain ideas of the Qumran sect could have percolated into Palestinian Judaism during the Arab period. To a very large

[1] Goitein, *Jews and Arabs*, p. 49.

[2] The word 'monk', *rāhib*, though commonly used for the Christian monks, is still unexplained. Geiger's derivation from Syr. *rabbā, rabbānā, 'doctor',* abbot', fails not only on the meaning, but mainly on the intrusive *h*. Possibly the word is simply Arabic and means 'fearing' (also in Syr. *rahīb*, 'fearful'); it may then be originally a translation of a phrase like *yir'ē el*, CDC xix. 20, or the Rabbinic *yĕrē shamayim*, 'pious'; cf. also *ḥăredhim bĕ-miẓwoth*, Ezra x. 3.

[3] In the Genizah story of Muhammad's Jewish companions (above, p. 123), Baḥīra appears as if he belonged to them, though his residence 'on a pillar in Balqīn' smacks more of a Christian Stylite.

extent the Muslim conquest meant to the Jews of the Middle East that liberation from 'their burden and the fetters that are upon them' which the Prophet had promised—at least for several centuries. The sectarians who came—as I suggest—in the wake of the victorious Muslim armies were thus proved right, and the 'Secrets of R. Simeon bar Yohai' go to show that they did what they could in order to bring this home to the widest circles. Being close to the ruling power, their prestige must have been tremendous. On the other hand, the first-century controversies had been forgotten by the Jews outside Arabia, and the struggle against Minim and Gnosticism had long ceased. The new-comers could thus be received without hesitation, and their ideas were absorbed to some extent in works like *Pirqe R. Eliezer*, while some of their halakhic tenets found acceptance in certain circles. Even their writings—as far as they still possessed any—could circulate, and so the two copies of CDC ultimately reached the Cairo Genizah. On the other hand, this percolation of ideas explains the very selective nature of the whole process. It is natural that their teachings should have found readiest acceptance in circles dissatisfied with the existing state of things. This explains their influence upon the emergent Karaite movement, in which perhaps the last remnants of the group were finally absorbed. The above account assumes, of course, that not all members of the group went as far as joining the Muslim community, as Ka'b had done.

There is nothing inherently improbable in the survival of a small religious community for centuries. We need only mention the Mandaeans and the Samaritans. While such communities in general tend to lose their vitality and militancy, they experience revivals. Moreover, where the existence of a closely related yet hostile group keeps such a community on the alert, the original militancy may last for a long time. The theory enounced in this chapter does therefore not favour any particular dating of the original Qumran community, though of course a later date makes the supposed period of survival shorter, and thereby more probable. This theory would also explain why contemporary Jewish sources are silent about the sect: during the Talmudic period it was outside the field of interest, and for the fifth–seventh centuries our sources

INDEX OF PASSAGES FROM THE DEAD SEA SCROLLS

ZADOKITE DOCUMENTS

DISCIPLINE SCROLL

PESHER HABAKKUK

THANKSGIVING SCROLL

WARS SCROLL

OTHER WRITINGS

SUBJECT INDEX